The Enchanted World
FABLED LANDS

The Enchanted World

FABLED LANDS

by the Editors of Time-Life Books

The Content

Chapter One

Journeys into Wonder · 6

An Enchanted Archipelago · 32

Chapter Two

Realms of Eternal Night · 48

Daring the Dark · 76

Chapter Three

A Parting of Worlds · 90

The Countess of the Fountain · 120

Time-Life Books · Alexandria, Virginia

Chapter One

T
Journeys into Wonder

he way of the traveler was, at best, uncertain when the earth was rough and young. Lands charged with magic lay hidden in the folds of the countryside, in the depths of the sea, even in the white fields of the clouds, sometimes visible and sometimes not. So shifting were the borders of these lands that a bend in a road, or a wave in the ocean, or the foot of a rainbow where it touched the ground, might prove a gateway for unsuspecting mortals. No one could tell when he might step from his own safe world across a border he could not see into a place where he would be a stranger, and all the life he had lived among his own kind would be as nothing.

Even the surface of still water might prove a portal to adventure, as an Arab tale reveals. The story concerns a young chieftain powerful enough to be called Sultan. His tribe was rich in the glossy horses that were the Arabs' pride, in camels, in goats and in slaves. The Sultan's stronghold, high in the hills above the desert called Rub' al Khali – or "Empty Quarter" – was crowded with rugs, with vessels of silver and coffers of ivory and bronze. The Sultan was a skilled warrior, wise in the ways of the world around him: He could tell time by the position of the sun; he could tell direction by observing the patterns of the stars as they wheeled in the clear night skies.

A practical man, the Sultan had little patience with fanciful tales. He therefore permitted himself to laugh one day when a pious elder of his tribe made reference to the legend of the Prophet Muhammad, who, it was said, rode through all the seven heavens on the back of al-Buraq – a beast that had the head of a woman, the body of a mule and a peacock's tail – to stand at last before the throne of God. The journey, according to the legend, lasted no more than the tenth part of a night.

Silence fell when the Sultan laughed: This was blasphemy. But the old man who had spoken remained unperturbed.

"Lord," he said, "would you see how swiftly a mortal man might travel?"

Diverted, the chieftain nodded his assent. The elder rose from the rug where he sat; he poured water into a golden bowl and murmured over it. Then he offered the bowl to his chief.

The Sultan stared down into the water and saw nothing but the shimmer of the gold that held it. He bent closer. Shapes appeared in the gilded depths; a miniature city formed itself in the liquid – not a for-

No one could tell where the portals to other worlds lay. A Sultan once looked
deep into a golden vessel filled with clear water; when he raised his head
again, he found himself on an unknown shore at the beginning of a new life.

tress city like his own massive aerie, but a sunny, whitewashed town, graced with high domes and slender towers, fringed by green palms and lapped by a gentle sea. Entranced, the Sultan bent closer still, until his face touched the cool water.

At that instant, it seized him. Down he went into the water; roaring filled his ears and darkness his eyes. He struggled slowly, as in a dream, pushing against rolling swells; his mouth opened, and he tasted salt.

As quickly as he had been caught, he was freed: His head broke the surface; his feet found footing again. Gasping for breath, he blinked the water from his eyes.

He stood chest-deep in the sea he had seen in the bowl, facing a sandy shore fringed with green; behind, the white walls of the city rose, set against towering clouds. The air was warm and very still.

He waded ashore, a stranger in a strange land. But someone awaited him. In the shadows of the palms, a young woman stood, a pale, pretty, dark-eyed woman. She regarded him gravely for some moments; then she smiled.

"You are the man from the sea," she said. "It was foretold that this day you would come to me to be my husband. I am the daughter of the goldsmith." She put out her hand to him, and at her touch the memories of his own life faded until they were only pale images, no more than glimpses of a childhood lived long ago.

The goldsmith's daughter led him into a coastal town not unlike those that bordered his domain in his own world. Dusty date palms lined its dirt streets; behind the palms, high, blank walls rose – silent façades masking the busy lives within.

"What country is this, lady?" asked the Sultan, who was a sultan no more.

"Why, this is the Country," she replied.

"Has it no name?"

"It needs no name."

"Who foretold that I would rise from the sea today?"

"My mother," she said, with a glance of surprise. "Our husbands always come from the sea and return to the sea when they die. Our mothers tell us the day."

The Sultan thought of men he had known, men who had disappeared without warning or explanation. He said nothing; there seemed nothing to say.

The goldsmith's daughter paused by a high wooden gate and rang a bell. At once, the gate swung open into the courtyard of the goldsmith's house. Here, all was shady, lush and cool. A fountain played in the center of the tiled court, and at the fountain's edge, the goldsmith stood, a tall man robed in fine white linen. He greeted the Sultan with equanimity; indeed, his words had the ring of ritual. "Welcome, my son from the sea," he said.

Thus was the Arabian ruler received into a family in a world he did not know. A fatalist, he accepted his lot – and indeed, his lot was not a hard one. The daughter of the goldsmith was beautiful, and her nature was gentle; the goldsmith himself was a rich man, and the quarters he had built for his daughter and his son-in-law were airy rooms, opening onto the courtyard.

So the Sultan married the goldsmith's daughter, according to the custom of the country, and he took up his father-in-law's craft: The crucible, the anvil and the graver of the goldsmith replaced the spear and sword of the Sultan's youth.

He was happy in that place. After a year, his wife bore him a daughter, as dark-eyed as she; by the time the girl was walking, another had been born. His wife bore a third child a year later, but this child died. The birth killed the mother.

After the burial was finished and the wails of mourning were stilled, late on an afternoon when his daughters were quiet in the care of their nurses, the young widower stood alone in the courtyard, spent with sorrow and numb with grief. A step sounded on the tiles; he raised his eyes to meet the gaze of his father-in-law.

"The gate stands open, son of the sea," the goldsmith said.

The younger man understood that, by the custom, he must seek his own death. He nodded dully. Then he walked out of the gate and into the dusty streets of the town. No one appeared. No voice called farewell to him. Through the bordering palms he walked, across the hot sand. Without hesitation, he waded into the welcoming sea, which tugged at his robes, drawing him onward until the waters closed over his head. He raised his face to catch the last of the light.

When he did so, he saw not watery shafts but the stone walls of the fortress chamber of his youth, exactly as he had left them years before; even the patches of sun on the floor were the same. In his hands he held a golden bowl.

Across its rim, the dim eyes of the elder of his tribe met his own.

"Have you journeyed long, lord?" the old man asked.

"For many years."

"For seconds only," said the elder. "For the space between one breath and the next. As the Prophet knew, there are places where time marches to a different rhythm from that made by the rising and setting of our sun."

What country he had entered through the water in the golden bowl, the Sultan could not say. He never found it again; nor did he ever learn the fate of the children he had fathered. All he knew from his adventure was that another world besides his own existed, a world whose patterns and rules were different, and where he had been allowed no more than the briefest sojourn. He had returned only with memories and with a longing that never left him.

Such ventures as the Sultan's were not uncommon once. Tale after tale was told of men and women who crossed the boundaries of their own world into lands most folk had not even dreamed of; tale after tale recorded the incursions of other-worldly beings onto the solid-seeming ground held by humankind. Such stories told of hazards. The passageways between the worlds were always shifting and were watched by guardians terrifying to the mortal soul. And the tales always had an elegiac tone: The old lands were fast disappearing; the gateways between them and the new, human-ruled earth were shutting one by one. For all the danger, adventurers sought the lands of enchantment while they could. And for many centuries those

lands were accessible, glimmering at the edge of vision, just over the horizon, or hidden but capable of being found.

Seafarers and coast dwellers, for instance, told of wonderful island worlds. Off the coast of Sicily, in the Strait of Messina, sometimes could be seen the cloud palaces of the Fata Morgana, a creation of the sorceress Morgan le Fay. Swedes spoke of Gummer's Ore, which sank and rose in the sea, surfacing before heavy storms and bringing with it great shoals of fish; some folk said Gummer's Ore sheltered a sea monster whose rising could founder a ship. The Scots spoke of Heather-Bleather, a fog-shrouded isle near the Orkneys that was ruled by seal men; those enchanted creatures, which sometimes took seal shape and sometimes human form, stole human brides, who never were seen among their own kind again.

The most haunted of seas lay off Ireland's west coast, where the presence of the old sea-god Manannan Mac Lir lingered so strongly that even in Christian times people reported seeing him skimming above the foam on his enchanted horse. Manannan's waters were realms of mystery. On them floated isles bearing castles made of glass, countries where the trees bore golden apples, lands peopled by giants and by monsters no mortal could describe. From these islands sometimes came the beings of Faerie, who ventured to human shores to tempt mortals away. Thus Irishmen sang of Connla, son of Conn of the Hundred Battles, whose heart was stolen by a fairy woman, for reasons no one could tell. Connla stood among his fellow warriors on the shore the day she came to take him. At her signal, he left his home and people, unprotesting. He sailed away in a crystal boat, moving steadily west across the waves, where the sun laid a track of gold over the ocean; he was swallowed into that brightness, and in the mortal world he was seen and heard no more.

Manannan's islands and his people were beautiful and perilous. Irishmen longed for the beauty and braved the peril, as the Irish *immrama* – voyage tales – tell. In their little coracles of hide-covered wickerwork, the adventurers sailed west into the sun; the men would be gone a year or two years or three; and those who returned told of wonders.

Such a tale was that of the island of Hy-Breasail, whose elusive manifestations charmed sailors for centuries. The island, which appeared to shimmer off the high headland of Killybegs on Ireland's western shore, was a phantom, according to the traveling cleric Gerald of Wales. It mocked those who sought it by vanishing beneath the waves as they approached. The island could be moored to the surface, Gerald thought, if a sailor fired a burning arrow into its soil. Fire, he said, would destroy the magic that controlled the island because fire was "the holiest of elements, being a witness of the secrets of the heavens."

Many were the sailors who saw Hy-Breasail from afar; only one, named Kirwan, claimed to have landed there. He was a young man of the Aran Islands who found himself fogbound one winter day while fishing for herring; a merchant sloop plucked him from the sea, but it too be-

The Irish told of ocean islands that were sometimes visible and sometimes not. Landing on one such isle, called Hy-Breasail, sailors found that their watch fires called forth demons.

13

A man among gods

The earliest mortals to leave their own world, storytellers said, were people who visited the heavens and conversed with the gods. One of these was Hadding, Prince of Denmark.

Hadding's early life was hard. His father was killed and his throne usurped by a Norwegian lord; the boy was sent by his countrymen into Sweden for safety and for training in the arts of war. When he was grown, he returned to Denmark to avenge his father's death.

But Hadding was young still; his venture failed, and he was wounded. When all seemed lost, a stranger came to his aid – a one-eyed sea rover who took him, unconscious, to his own home. There, in a high, thatched hall, the Danish Prince was healed of his wounds. When he was strong again, the sea rover told him that he would fight a lion and slay it. He must drink the lion's blood and absorb its strength for victory, the one-eyed man said. Then he set Hadding behind him on a horse, covered him with a cloak, and conveyed the Prince to his own country in darkness.

Events ran true to their prophesied course. Hadding gained the lion's strength. Men flocked to him. He killed the invader and freed Denmark, taking his rightful place as King.

He knew where his good fortune had come from. On the ride toward Denmark, he had peered out from the concealing cloak. He saw the clouds racing around him, and far below, he saw the gray and rippling sea. Asgard, the gods' sky country, had sheltered him. His benefactor was one-eyed Odin, All-Father of the Norsemen.

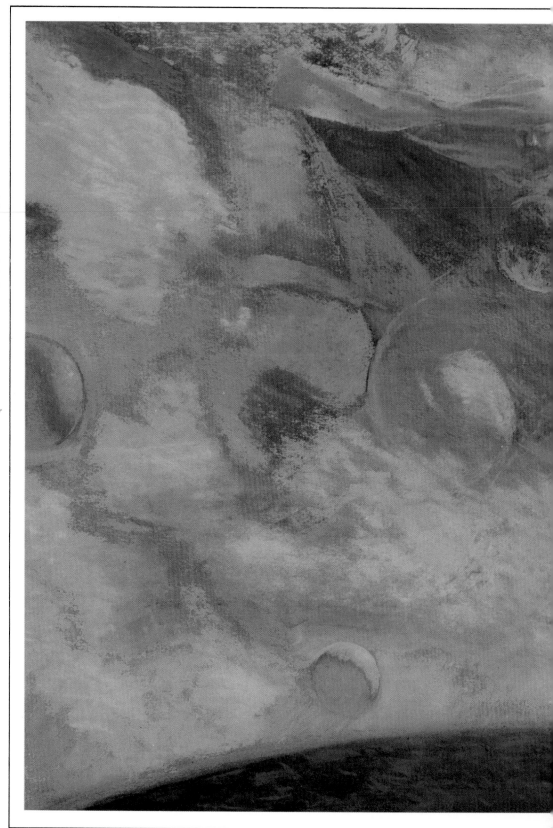

came lost in the blinding mist, drifting aimlessly in the windless air. At length, the ship anchored off an unknown shore, and the fog dissolved, drifting away in tatters to reveal a rolling landscape where sheep and cattle grazed. Close to the shore stood a castle, little more than a stone watchtower. The men called, but no sentry answered; the fortress stood silent and shuttered, apparently deserted.

Because night was drawing in, the men made camp on the quiet shore. They unloaded supplies and built a campfire. But the moment flint struck steel to light the kindling, chaos erupted. A banshee wail rose from the ground, and brightness exploded in the air. Clouds of shadow shapes leaped above their heads, dancing a maniac, howling dance. Terrified, Kirwan and the sailors retreated to their ship to keep watch on the ghost fires that played around the island and its tower.

The first light of morning brought peace. And when the early sun shone on the tower stones, it revealed an open gate. An aged man shuffled through this portal, squinting at the ship offshore and gesturing. He was unarmed. The captain of the sloop sent a few of his men and Kirwan to shore in a dinghy.

According to Kirwan's account, the old man – soon joined by other elders – welcomed them with gratitude and told them they had saved his island – long trapped in invisibility by the spells of enemies – by bringing fire to it. The flames had broken the enchantment that bound him and his people.

Even years later, when he himself was old, Kirwan would show the coins the old man had given him then – gold and silver, battered beyond recognition. But he could not tell who the old man was or what enemy had enspelled him. The sailors were the last humans ever to set foot on Hy-Breasail; when they sailed for home, the island retreated once more behind clouds of mist, showing itself, like other fabled kingdoms, only in images that swiftly appeared and as swiftly faded.

A peculiar elusiveness distinguished many territories of enchantment as the centuries wore on, so that tales about them survive mostly as fragments, records of fleeting moments in human experience. The 12th Century English monk William of Malmesbury reported such a moment. A French cleric, whom William knew, was shown, while traveling in Italy, a mountain that the peasants said hid the treasures of the Emperor Octavian – heir to Julius Caesar. Curious, the monk and his fellows climbed the mountain and entered a cave that they found near the summit. They followed a twisting passage that broadened to a road littered with human bones. The road ended at a great underground lake, black as night and spanned by a bridge of brass; its far end was guarded by two statues of knights wrought from gold and mounted on golden horses. Reckless with avarice, the men stepped onto the bridge. At once, its near side dipped into the dark water, its far side soared toward the cavern roof and a hideous gonging filled the air. The monks fled, taking nothing but a silver chalice one of them found on the road among the bones.

They returned the next day, to discover that guardians had been set upon the treasure: Twisted, charred bodies, with eyes of flame, hissed and gobbled at the cave mouth, reaching with eager claws for the human intruders. Demons, the monks said, and left the place forever.

That brief report was all that was known of Octavian's buried territory. It differed little from the stories of other kings and warriors lying frozen in mountain caverns in the company of their fellows – sleeping until their countrymen should call them again.

Thus, said the Germans, the Holy Roman Emperor and Crusader Frederick Barbarossa lived on in a limestone cave beneath the forested Kyffhäuser mountains; he sat at a stone table through which – after long centuries – the red beard that gave him his name had grown. The Irish hero Finn Mac Cumal slumbered in a cave with his company of warriors. It was foretold that three blasts on the horn called Dord Fiann would wake him one day, and he would restore Ireland's glory. Various caves in Glamorganshire in Wales were said to hide King Arthur and his companions. And near Cardiganshire, beneath a hazel tree on a lonely moor, stone steps led deep into the earth to a vast cavern where slept Owen Lawgoch – "Red Hand" – with a sword of the ancient British Kings in his hand, and armored men and gold all around him. Many folk believed that this venerable warrior – said to be one of Britain's defenders against Saxon invasions – would rise again to lead the nation.

Legends relate that these enchanted territories were occasionally seen by farmers or itinerant smiths, who stumbled upon them accidentally. Sometimes, according to the stories, the intruders would partly awaken the old ones. A voice from the shadows would ask, "Is it time?" and the terrified human would reply, "Rest, thou, the time is not yet come," thus sending the ghostly sleepers back to their rest.

But tales of heroes sleeping in enchanted caverns are cloudy enough to shake belief. They are like the stories of lost countries such as Lyonnesse, a kingdom at the tip of Cornwall, which was engulfed by the sea. Only its mountain peaks – the Scilly Islands – remained in view; the only voices left were those of its church bells, which rang beneath the waves on windy nights. Such stories too often seem the inventions of men and women anxious to explain the mysteries around them in human terms, populating mountain caverns with their own kind and giving a human name to the voices rising from the waves.

The voices were real; the life that breathed in the stone was real. But it was not human. Rather, it was the last breath of races far older than the human one.

The earliest people knew this. In Greece and in northern lands as well, they told tales of an age when old gods still walked upon the earth; these gods, said storytellers, did not hesitate to interfere in the affairs of young humankind. Sometimes they took men and women into their own realms in the hills and valleys of the clouds, showing them wonders – such as gold-thatched halls floating in the blue and horses that could fly.

The mountains of England, Ireland, Wales and Germany hid ancient warriors—men sealed

away for centuries in the realms of sleep until their countrymen called for their aid.

In Ireland, people told of the Tuatha Dé Danann, an ancient, kingly, warrior race, whom some called old gods and some called fairies. The Tuatha had vanished from the face of Ireland when mortals settled there, but these old ones did not die. They simply retreated. Their lands lay under the sea and under the earth; indeed, some of Ireland's low, green hills were known as the gateways to their kingdoms.

Behind those gates, the secret, vibrant world of the Tuatha went on. In it were enchanted treasures and old magics unfathomable to mortals. Its life was lighted by a different sun and marked by time patterns different from those of humankind.

The Tuatha were a protean people. They could take the form of tall and beautiful men and women, but if they wished, they could also venture into mortal territory in the guise of swans or ravens or even the winds on the waters or the waves in the sea. And their dealings with humanity were as changeable as they themselves, a baffling mixture of beneficence and hostility. The Tuatha protected the fertility of the mortals' fields, it was said; sometimes in those early days they married mortal men and women, so that some Irish families could boast of fairy blood. Yet they were a race imbued with savage power, and they were capable of mounting ferocious assaults on the usurpers of their land.

To guard against the Tuatha's magic, the Irish surrounded themselves with rules and protective words and definitions; the order they imposed on life served as a wall against the disorderly powers of their predecessors. But all of life could not be ordered, and not all Irishmen were willing to obey the rules that offered safety, as the tale of Nera tells:

Nera served Maeve, the warrior-queen of Connacht, and her husband, Ailill. His adventure began on Samain Eve, the night that divided summer and winter in Celtic lands. Samain was like other in-between times – dawn, dusk, midnight, year's end. At such chinks in time – periods outside definition – indefinable powers were loosed upon the world. On Samain Eve, wise folk stayed in their houses, knowing that the dead walked the night and that the warriors of the Tuatha were free to roam.

But some men dared the dark, and one was Nera, because of a challenge by Ailill the King, master of the Samain feasting.

Sitting in his firelit hall, Ailill looked down the ranks of his warriors lounging on their benches, sluggish with drink, and said that any man brave enough to tie a withe – a plait of twigs – around the ankle of a dead man hanging on the gallows outside the fortress should have his own gold-hilted sword. Nera took up the challenge.

Nera walked out of the hall, past the watchmen at the gates, down the sloping road that led away from the hill of Cruachan, the grassy mound where the fortress stood. Only a faint wind stirred the dead leaves on the trees; his footsteps were loud on the stone of the road as he made his way to the gallows tree. From a stout branch dangled the body of a thief who had been hanged the day before. No one had cut him down; no wise person touched a corpse on Samain Eve.

But Nera did. With cold and trembling

hands, he tied a withe around one stiffened leg. And when he had done so, a dull voice spoke above his head.

"Carry me to water," said the corpse. "I was thirsty when I died."

Having touched a corpse on the night of the dead, Nera was in its power. Without comment, he cut the body down; the legs wrapped around his waist and the cold arms around his neck. A guttural chuckle sounded in Nera's ear. "Forward," said the dead man. And Nera trudged along the road to a cluster of farmers' huts.

Although he was now the dead man's tool, he had acquired the corpse's vision, and so saw sights invisible to human eyes. The first hut he approached with his burden was walled against enemies by a lake of flame and the second by one of water. In those houses, the people had thrown out their waste and banked their hearth fires so as to give the walking dead no welcome. That was the custom in the region. The third house was dark; here, no protective measures had been taken. Nera entered it. The corpse climbed down from Nera's back, crawled across the dirt floor and gulped from a jug that stood by the hearth. After a time, it wiped its mouth. Then it spat water on the farmer and his wife, sleeping on their pallets. They withered and died where they lay. "Let that teach you to follow safe customs," said the corpse to Nera, its eyes gleaming with malevolence. "Take me back to my gallows. I will show you other sights."

So it did. When Nera had strung the body up again, he turned toward the fortress. Black smoke billowed in high towers above the ramparts. The gates stood open,

and flames licked at the lintels. In the fire glow was silhouetted a troop of warriors; they ran down the fortress road, and Nera saw that the severed heads of his companions were tethered to their belts. At the base of the hill of Cruachan, the company of raiders vanished into a cave mouth that suddenly yawned there.

Without a thought, Nera followed the company of warriors. He ran to the cave mouth and entered, not even glancing at the fortress burning above. Then he paused to catch his breath and get his bearings. At his back, the earth closed. Far away, the footsteps of the raiders dwindled into silence.

Having no choice, he walked forward along a track that twisted down between stone walls into the depths of the hill. He walked for what seemed to be hours, his way illuminated by a half-light that emanated from the rock itself. At last the track narrowed; it ended in a flight of stone steps that led to an archway in the rock.

In the archway, Nera halted and stared out over another country, spread before him as far as the eye could see. Above was a rosy sky where faint stars glittered in patterns he did not recognize. Below, silvered by the starlight, lay heavy-laden orchards and fields of high grain. This seemed to be a summer country. In the midst of the fields stood a palace, and it was nothing like the round, wooden halls of Ailill and the other Irish Kings. Its walls were of a glassy stone that caught and held the starlight; slender towers adorned the walls, and from the windows, light streamed

The drowned kingdom of Ker-Ys

Not all hidden lands were territories of fairy peoples; some held mortals caught in enchantment. The Breton city of Ker-Ys, which long ago lay behind massive dikes on the western coast of Finistère, was destined to become such a place.

At one time, it was a rich city-kingdom, ruled by a man named Gralon. He had a beautiful daughter, Ahès, whom he dearly loved, never seeing the evil within her. Ahès had a passion for young men. One by one she seduced them; one by one, as she finished with them, her servants strangled them and threw their bodies into a gorge behind the city.

Of all the court, only one man suspected Ahès. He was Guénolé, her father's councilor. But he had no proof of her murderous ways, and dared not speak to the King.

A catastrophe finally loosened his tongue. One day, the city dikes were opened by a pale young man, clearly enspelled by Ahès. The sea poured into Ker-Ys, swirling through the streets and into the houses. From his palace, Gralon the King saw what had happened. He raced to the courtyard, leaped onto a horse, pulled Ahès up onto the saddle, and galloped away from the onrushing water. Guénolé galloped beside them. But the water was too swift. Caught in the surge, the horses flailed and struggled, and at last Guénolé spoke.

"Cast off the she-devil who clings to your saddle," he shouted. At his words, Ahès gave a hissing cry and threw herself into the waves. Instantly, the floodwaters ceased to rise. The King and his councilor turned to look at their city. It lay submerged – and there it would remain.

In later days, the Bretons said that Ker-Ys lived and would emerge from the sea again, when the right spell was pronounced. And they said that Ahès continued to haunt the region, a spirit of the sea whose pretty songs enticed sailors to their deaths off the shores of Finistère.

The gates into the dominions of Faerie were most likely to open at particular times
of year. When an Irish warrior named Nera touched a hanged man on the Eve of
Samain, the corpse spoke and guided him out of the territory of humankind.

out in golden shafts. In the distance, on mountains that loomed behind the fields and orchards, other castles glimmered.

An iron hand closed on Nera's arm. He turned to face a tall warrior, armored and helmeted in leather. The man's sword was drawn. With a jerk of his head, he signaled Nera to walk before him, and Nera obeyed. So he was taken from the scented orchards to the palace of the King.

In fact, no harm came to him. The King's hall was crowded, but there was no sign of the warriors Nera had seen carrying his companions' heads. The people in the hall appeared and disappeared around him, so many fireflies on a summer's night; only the King, a red-haired man, cloaked in scarlet, had substantiality. He regarded Nera with amusement: What had a Tuatha King to fear from a lone mortal in his realm? He had Nera put in the keeping of a woman and ordered him to work at carrying firewood for the palace.

That was a mistake. The fairy woman lived in a white house in a wood; she herself was slender and pale, as most of the Tuatha women were; her hair was as silvery as moonlight, and her eyes were the gray of a winter sea. They brightened when Nera was brought to her, for although he was not armored, he had the bearing of a warrior. He was a handsome and vigorous man.

The fairy woman and the mortal became lovers that night; Nera stayed in the white house the next day and night. The third night, the woman asked him how he had come to enter the kingdom, and he told her about the burning of Ailill's fortress and the opening of the cave at Cruachan. The woman hesitated for a moment; then she stroked his hair and laughed.

"Sometimes mortals are given vision," she said. "The burning has not happened yet; the King will take the fortress a year from now, if you do not prevent him."

"And how can he be prevented?"

"I will tell you if I have your oath that you will return to me – and to your child, whom I will bear."

Nera pledged himself to her, and the woman told what he must do: He must return to his own people and warn them.

"How can I return? I have been here for three days; the cave has shut."

"You have been here moments only; in Ailill's hall, the warriors still sit around the caldron at their Samain feast."

"How shall I prove that I speak true?"

"Take with you fruits of summer to your winter land," she replied. "At next Samain, when the cave opens once more, Ailill and his warriors must attack this kingdom, saving only me and our child. They must take the treasure that protects the realm, so that the King will lack the strength to destroy Ailill. The treasure is the King's golden diadem that rests in a well in the court of his palace. It is guarded by a lame man who rides the back of a blind man, and these Ailill's warriors must cut down."

Then the woman led Nera through the summery land to the well where the talisman crown rested, watched by its crooked guardians. She took him to the arch that was the gate to her land; she gave him wild garlic and primrose and golden fern to carry with him to the mortal world. And she

Nera saw a vision of his chief's fortress put to the torch by invaders. He
followed the warriors to an archway in a hillside, a door to an elder world.

reminded him of the oath he had given.

All happened as she said. When a year had passed and the gates to the Tuatha's realm opened at the Eve of Samain, Ailill and his men were waiting. They stormed the world under their world; they took away the golden crown and retreated to the air again; then the gateway in Cruachan closed. Nera stayed behind with the fairy woman and their child. He was never seen by his companions again.

Thus was a realm of Faerie shut away from mortal eyes. Tales of the cave of Cruachan continued to be told: how sometimes it opened, releasing ferocious birds that attacked both cattle and people, how fairy women emerged in wolf shape to steal sheep. But no one again walked into the cave and down the stone steps that led to the summer country of the Tuatha.

Although the Tuatha became more elusive, hundreds of years passed before men and women ceased to see them. The hidden fairy life flowed on; in their decline, the Tuatha remained beautiful and incomprehensibly changeable — now ally, now enemy — to those who trod the earth above them. Fear of them faded as their power faded, but no man or woman claimed to understand their ways, not even those who were brought into their world.

Centuries after Nera vanished into the hill of Cruachan, for instance, descendants of his people still ventured into other parts of Faerie — for reasons quite different from those that impelled Nera. These adventurers were the Fianna, the shining brotherhood that, under its chief, Finn Mac Cumal, guarded the Kings of Ireland.

It happened once that fourteen of the Fianna were stolen away, tricked into mounting a fairy horse. The horse swelled to giant size to carry them all and, with the ease of enchantment, galloped from the Fianna's pastures into the ocean, skimming over the waves until it disappeared.

As they were sworn to do, the Fianna sent a war band after the men. In a hide-covered coracle, captained by Finn, they sailed in the direction the horse had taken. They voyaged for some days before they sighted land — a place no one knew. Straight up from the foaming surf the island rose, a place of high, pockmarked cliffs, loud with the cries of sea birds. The Fianna steered their coracle into the shelter of a rocky cove, and Diarmuid, son of Donn, the bravest and the merriest of them, left the company to reconnoiter.

Diarmuid climbed up the cliff face, clinging to niches in the spray-slick rock and fighting off sea birds defending their nests. When he gained the top, he looked down. A toylike boat bobbed in the surf far below; all he could see of his companions were the small, pale ovals of their upturned faces. He waved to show that he was safe and turned inland.

A fair country lay spread out before him, flat and green and dotted with woods. In the midst of the meadows, a single tree stood, a mighty tree, thick of trunk and heavy of bough, and to this tree Diarmuid walked. Standing stones loomed among its serpentine roots, and at the base of one stone lay a well of water so limpid that it seemed to give off light. A drinking horn of gold hung beside the

In the land beneath the hill, Nera found a wonder: a crown hidden in
a guarded well. The crown was a talisman protecting that domain.

well. Diarmuid took it up and filled it from the well and raised it to his lips.

The horn was knocked from his hand before he could drink. Diarmuid spun around to face an enemy, a burly, white-bearded man, helmeted in gold and raising an unsheathed broadsword.

Quick as thought, Diarmuid drew his own sword. The two fought doggedly all that afternoon, while the tree shadows lengthened and the air grew cool and still. But at the moment twilight fell, the gold-helmeted knight vanished. Diarmuid was left alone, to watch through the night.

The battle was repeated the next day: The adversary appeared in the same baffling fashion, and disappeared as swiftly when night came. But the third evening, Diarmuid forestalled him: When the first star shone in the sky, he threw down his sword and flung himself at the enemy, wrapping his arms around the man's body.

Thus he joined the white beard in a plunge into the other world. The warrior leaped into the well, with Diarmuid clinging to him. For an instant, Diarmuid had an image of the twilight sky rimmed with black. Then the water closed over his head. Down and down the two men fell, and the world went dark for the Irishman.

He awoke alone. He lay on a broad plain near a wood; in the distance, the towers of a golden city rose under a sunny sky. His enemy was nowhere to be seen.

But other adversaries waited. Shouting war cries, a company of men burst from the wood with murder in their voices. Diarmuid met them with nothing more than his hunting knife, but he was a dangerous opponent with that knife. He moved as quickly as a cat; one man fell, and then another and another. In his battle fury, Diarmuid danced among them, circling for the final kill. The last man fell—but not before knocking Diarmuid to the ground. Once again, the dark closed in.

A low voice roused him. A silk-cloaked man bent over him, and the man's eyes were gentle. "Rise, mortal hero, and come with me," he said. "I will take you to a place where you will be healed, for you have done a great deed for my people this day."

Then he led Diarmuid into the shining city, where he found the men who had sailed with him and the fellows of their company who had vanished across the sea, riding the enchanted horse. All of them, said the white-bearded man, had been brought to this place—called Under-Wave—to champion the Tuatha against their enemies in a time when the Tuatha could triumph only with human aid. All of them had fought, as Diarmuid had fought.

But who were the enemies and what was the war? The story did not say. It said only that Diarmuid and the Fianna had been called out of their own world to help the warriors of another, weaker world. The mortal men, like so many before and after them, had been given a glimpse—and only a glimpse—of the hidden life beneath earth and sea. When Diarmuid's wounds had healed, the Fianna found themselves back in their own pastures by their own shores, and none could say how they got there. Nor did they ever find the well and its guardian or the land of Under-Wave again. 🐍

Any opening in sea or land—a whirlpool, a lake, a cavern, a well— might mark the borders of enchantment. A well caught Finn's man Diarmuid: He challenged the guardian of the water and plunged to adventure.

An Enchanted Archipelago

This is the tale of Maelduin of Ireland, who sailed out of his own world onto seas of wonder, finding islands that held both danger and delight.

Maelduin's early life was spent in the eastern part of the country; he was reared as one of the four sons of the King and Queen of that region. The boys, having been brought up "in one cradle, on one breast and in one lap," say the chroniclers, were extraordinarily close. But Maelduin was not one of the brothers, as he was told when he reached manhood. He was the son of a dead man, Ailill Edge of Battle, a chieftain of the people of Owen, by the shore of the western sea. The son had been sent into fosterage in his infancy for his own safety.

When Maelduin discovered who he was, he journeyed to his father's homeland with his foster brothers. There, he found out how his father had died — trapped in a church that sea raiders put to the torch. Grim-faced on learning this, Maelduin stood among the charred stones and swore vengeance. That was the first step on a journey destined to last years.

Within a few months, Maelduin had built a ship. It was fashioned according to the instructions of a wizard and was shielded by his charms. The wickerwork frame was covered with hardened oxhide; the crew, as the wizard had ordered under pain of cursing, was exactly seventeen men, all companions of Maelduin. His foster brothers had not joined the crew, but on the day the many-colored sail was hoisted and the coracle pushed off the shingle into the sea, they followed, shouting to be taken aboard. Maelduin at first refused because of the curse, but when the brothers of his childhood flung themselves into the sea and swam after him, he had the ship put about and he pulled them aboard, lest they drown.

The red-hued vessel sailed west all that day and into the night, searching for the island of Leix, which was the sea raiders' stronghold. Maelduin saw its outline at midnight and heard, floating across the sea, the voices of the raiders, raucous at their feasting. He signaled. The ship slipped toward the shore.

As the coracle approached the shallows, a voice rang out. It was the raiders' chief, shouting triumphantly to his men: "I lead you all. I slew Ailill Edge of Battle, the bonny fighter, and no one has dared to avenge him after all these years."

Maelduin, standing in the bow, drew his spear. Before the coracle reached the shore, however, storm clouds boiled up and blotted out the stars, wind howled down from the north, and great waves

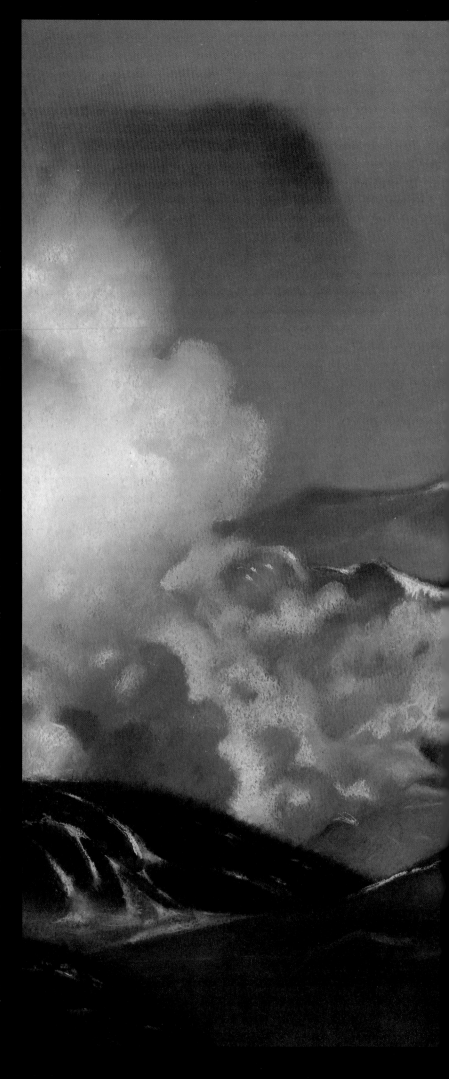

seized the ship in an irresistible grip.

During the night, the company was driven away from the raiders' shore, far out into the unknown ocean. Two days passed; on the morning of the third, the storm died, and the warriors, stiff and sore, found themselves on a glassy sea, rimmed at the horizon with the humped backs of scattered islands.

"It is because of you that the way is lost," Maelduin said to his foster brothers. He ordered his helmsman to steer for a nearby group of islands, thinking to find shelter. The coracle touched the pebbled shore of a deep cove. High cliffs rose behind this beach – cliffs edged with black shapes that for a moment stood motionless as stones. Then the shapes began to move. With no sound but a soft rustling of their legs, they swarmed down the cliff-side. The creatures were huge ants, as big as foals. On they came, feelers waving, mandibles clacking. Maelduin and his men pushed off, spun the coracle around with mighty oar-strokes and headed out to sea.

In the next days of sailing, while their store of provisions dwindled, they sheered away from island after island. Strange beasts roared at them from promontories; they saw lands where the sand was marked with the hoofprints of horses – each hoofprint the size of their vessel's sail. They glided near a shore where a horror prowled, a beast that seemed to revolve within its skin. It howled at them in fury, then grasped stones in its claws and hurled them at the retreating coracle.

Driven by hunger, they put in on an island thick with apple trees and swirling with steam. The ground was hot under their feet and pitted with holes that led to underground caverns. There, amid flickering flames, lurked scarlet swine that fed upon

he apples. The men took what fruit
they could reach easily and fled.

Finally they landed on the shore
of a mountain island that promised a
haven. On its crest, white ramparts
reached into the clouds, and in the
shelter of the scarp white houses
stood. The warriors advanced up
the slope. They hailed the fortress,
but the only answer was the echo
of their voices.

Wondering if the inhabitants
were huddled indoors, they entered
a house, passing into an airy courtyard whose walls were hung with
treasure: rows of brooches worked in
filigree, golden neck torques,
bejeweled swords. No man or woman greeted them, but the place was
welcoming. In the center of the
yard, a great table stood, laden with
bread and ale and smoked meat. Surrounding the table were tall stone
pillars, and on one of these pillars
sat a cat — an ordinary white cat by all
outward signs. Evidently it was the
guardian of the house. Maelduin
asked, "Is this food for us?" The cat
stared at him with round, unblink-
ing eyes. Then it began to play,
hopping from pillar to pillar with the
ease of any common cat.

So the men feasted, and when
they had done, they slept. On a pil-
ar, the cat curled up and slept too.

In the morning, the company ate
again, then made ready to leave the
place. Maelduin's eldest foster
brother took a golden neck torque
from the hall as booty, although
Maelduin told him sharply to leave
it and not abuse the laws of hospital-
ty. The cat hissed a warning.

The man ignored them both.
Clutching the treasure, he strode
through the courtyard. He did not
look back and therefore did not see
how the white cat arched and leaped,
how it sailed through the air like an
arrow. He had not time even to cry

out as the animal shot through his body, spitting fire, and made of him a tall torch of burning flesh that collapsed and melted as his companions watched, frozen by fear.

Maelduin picked up the golden torque, put it back in its place and asked the cat's pardon. He led his men to the coracle to continue a voyage that had no direction and no foreseeable end.

Magic seemed to reign on every island they approached. They passed close to one isle neatly bisected by a fence of brass where a shepherd stood. On one side of the fence, black sheep grazed; on the other, white; when a sheep crossed out of its own territory, its color changed. To test the magic, Maelduin threw a staff onto the shore among the black sheep; the staff turned to ebony. Terrified, the company sped away. Next, their voyage took them past islands where huge cows grazed, then past an island where a giant shouted threats across the water and said that he was the miller who turned the mill of hell.

After days of noise and menace, they arrived at a quiet island, green

with yew and willow trees. Among
the trees, a throng of people moved,
people hooded and robed in black,
and from this throng came a soft
keening, broken by muffled sobs.

After Maelduin had brought the
coracle ashore, the company cast
lots to determine who would venture
among these mourners to ask the
cause of their sorrow and discover
what this place might be. The lot fell
to the second of Maelduin's foster
brothers. The young man leaped
onto the sand and strode into the
woods. A black-robed woman
touched his hand; before the eyes of
his fellows, he trembled and his flesh
darkened. The woman cast her arm
around his shoulders. When she removed it, he had become a cloaked
and hooded specter, indistinguishable from the rest of the throng.
Maelduin sent men after him, in-
structing them not to speak with the
mourners or even look at them di-
rectly. But by then, the brother had
disappeared. He had become one
with this island world, separate forever from his own kind.

The warriors sailed onward, drifting with wind and current through a region where every land was strange to them. They came to a high island crowded with fairy people who gave them enchanted ale to drink; the ale blessed them with sleep for days while the coracle continued its wanderings. They sailed by an island that was hardly more than a rock; on it, a white-bearded hermit crouched. He gave them words of prophecy: All of them would reach home, he said, save one. They crossed a sea whose surface seemed a frail membrane, barely substantial enough to support the coracle; beneath the bow, in the transparent water, was a country of rolling hills where sheep grazed and mighty strongholds loomed. Later, they reached an isle where a fountain played rainbow-like over the land; in that clear, aerial stream, silver salmon leaped and played. The men speared the fish and ate their fill. When they resumed their journey, they took a store of salmon with them.

They sailed on into a night where the moon made a ribbon in the water and the stars sparkled on the black sea. Here, no islands lay on the horizon or loomed near. But they saw a gleaming tower in the distance, and toward this the Irishmen steered.

When they drew near, they were

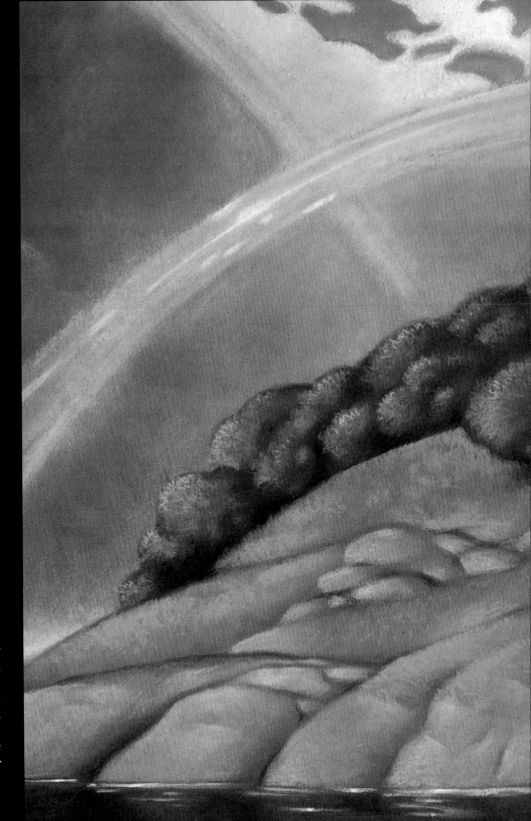

struck into silence. The tower was a column of silver, rising straight from the water, so high was it that they could not see its summit. It appeared to hold up the sky. Draped around the base and floating lightly on the rippling sea was a net of silver, seemingly made of stars. The coracle slid through the sparkling mesh; one of the men struck it with the edge of his spear blade, tearing away a piece of the fabric to offer as proof of the journey if ever he should gain his home again. A voice chimed down from the heights of the silver pillar then, but it spoke in an unknown tongue, and the words had no meaning to the company.

So the journey among mysteries continued. In all, Maelduin and his men sailed for more than three years, now fleeing from danger, now resting on islands where elfin folk lived. Had not the wizard's curse been lifted, they might have voyaged through this enchanted archipelago until they died.

Their release came with the loss of the third of Maelduin's foster brothers, the last of those who had brought the curse upon the ship. He disappeared on an island of mad folk, people who laughed without cease and without meaning. When he had vanished from the company, a falcon appeared over the sea, winging strongly to the southeast.

They followed the bird day and

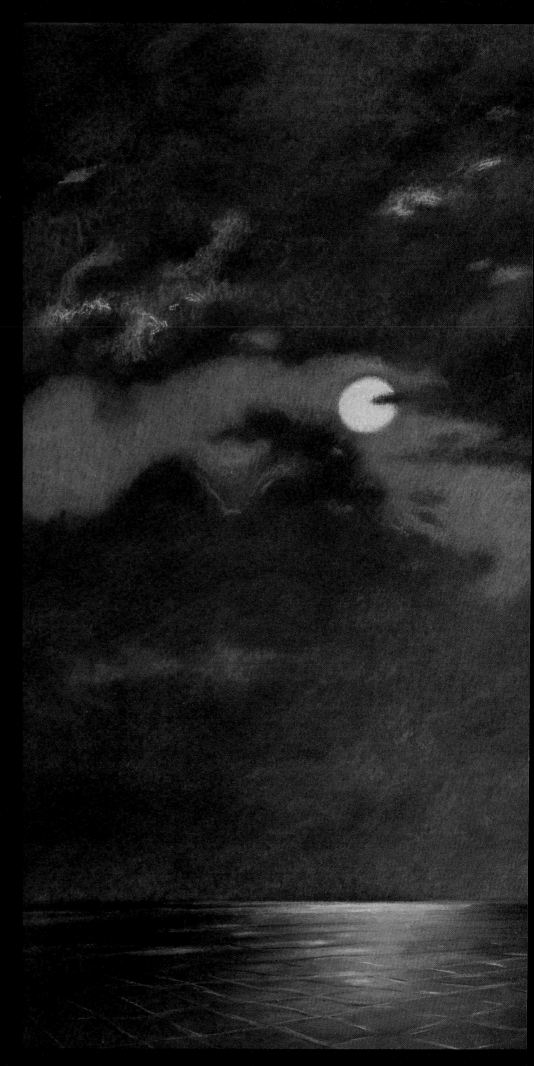

night. It led them across the water
and through clouds and mist, past
some border that they could not see,
and finally to a place that was famil-
iar – the island of the sea raiders.
There they beached the coracle and
marched up to the fortress where,
long ago, they had heard the raiders'
chief boast of murder. But now they
heard him speak of Maelduin as a
man who braved the unknown, as
a warrior he would wish to make his
friend. And when the chief saw the
company, he welcomed them. Maelduin, who had grown in wisdom
through his trials, forgave the man
and offered his hand in peace.

When the adventurers reached
Ireland again, they told of their
strange and aimless voyage, of the
uncharted storm that had driven
them across the sea, of the island
world they had found, filled with
creatures they could not recognize
and subject to laws they could not
understand, and they presented the
silver net for proof. So wonderful
was their recounting that a man
named Aed Finn, who was then the
chief poet of that poetry-loving
people, made it into a song to do
the company honor. Thus the voyage of Maelduin lived in words for
a thousand years.

Chapter Two

T Realms of Eternal Night

The longships of the Northmen ranged far once: south to France and Sicily, west to Britain, eastward to the Russian coasts. They breached seas where ships had never sailed before, touching shores never named. And they sailed older oceans in search of the kingdoms of the first worlds—dark and windy wastelands not meant for men, ancient realms ruled by generations of the dead.

Gorm, King of Denmark, was one of the venturers. He was fired by the words of a man named Thorkil, a sea rover who had sailed to Iceland and beyond, who had skirted seas of night beyond Finnmark's North Cape and brought back tales of treasure hidden in giant-guarded caves. Gorm chose to find those lands himself—not for gold, said the chroniclers, but for glory—and he made Thorkil the guide and captain of his company. All through one winter, therefore, after the crops were in, Gorm's ships were built under Thorkil's direction. Three long keels of oak were laid on the winter grass and fitted with stems and sterns and hulls of overlapping strakes, hide-covered to provide protection from the ocean spray. Three masts were stepped in their oaken kerlings; three snarling dragons' heads were fitted to the three prows. The chroniclers claimed that the ships were larger even than the *Great Dragon*, a famous thirty-five bencher that Harald Hardrada used in his assaults on Britain. Gorm's vessels, they said, were fifty-benchers, each carrying a hundred oarsmen.

And on a spring morning, under bright skies alive with racing clouds, the three great ships, their keels reddened with the blood of sacrifice, slid groaning and smoking over log rollers into the sea. The company that sailed in them was a proud one—three hundred warriors armed with Frankish swords and silver-ornamented battle-axes. In leather bags beneath their rowing benches were provisions to last months.

With a brisk wind at their backs, they glided through the protected channels of the Kattegat and Skagerrak between Denmark and the Scandinavian mainland, soon reaching the open sea. The helmsman in the leading ship was Thorkil, a

T·HOWELL·'85

heavy-set man with the leathery skin and sun-bleached hair of the sailor. Northward he took them, clinging to the land while he could, past the towering mountains that framed the Norwegian fjords, past Helgeland and Finnmark and into the vast gray ocean. He steered by sun and stars, by the movements of the shoaling fish and the flights of the sea birds, by a hundred other signs that seamen knew.

But as weeks became months and the three ships continued steadily north, the seaman's signs began to fade. The days grew shorter and darker. No fish swam around the ships' hulls; no birds cried in the sky. The wind dropped. No moon shone: For most of the day, the only light besides the glimmer of the mast lanterns came from the stars overhead, and even these were strangely sparse and dim — more frightening than comforting. They had entered the realm of night now, ruled by beings who were not mortal.

They moved in a shroud of darkness, in an envelope of silence marred only by the creak of the oars in the oarlocks and the splash of the blades in the water. Yet they were not alone. A time came when they could hear, far away, above the sullen hiss of the swells, the crashing of surf on shore. Thorkil steered them toward the sound.

"This is the outpost," he said, his voice carrying in the air. "Take no more than you need. Only that much is allowed."

But the company hardly heeded him, and even Gorm the King shrugged. These were people bred on the custom of the *strandhogg*, the shore raids Norsemen conducted whenever provisions in their longships ran low. They beached the ships in a rocky inlet rimmed by pasture where cattle — obviously innocent of human contact — crowded toward them in the dimness, regarding them with large, curious eyes. Over the side and into the mass of cattle the seamen swarmed, slaughtering with brutal efficiency. They killed and butchered not just enough animals for a meal, but all the animals, and they loaded so many carcasses into their vessels that the ships rode perilously low in the water.

Retribution was swift. As soon as they pushed away from the shore, huge shapes, difficult to see in the half-light, pressed close to them, bellowing in an unknown tongue. The creatures were monsters, the men said later, but no one could describe them. Such was their power that the vessels began to rock violently, shipping water and threatening to capsize. Then Thorkil's voice sounded clear above the roar.

"What is the price of the slaughter?" the captain cried.

"A life from each ship," came the reply.

The price was given. Thorkil drew lots to choose the victims. Three warriors were thrust from the longships into the shallows, where the shadow creatures waited. Then the ships drew away, trailed by the agonized screams of the men left behind.

In the hours that followed, Thorkil issued instructions to be passed from man to man, and now his words were heeded. They would come to a borderland, he said, a place ruled by a living giant. It was a place of testing, and beyond it lay the treasure lands of the old gods. He gave them the charm that would protect them on the passage through the worlds: "Speak no word, except among yourselves. Eat no food, except your own. Take nothing that is not yours to take."

As he spoke, the stars winked out. The adventurers sailed for hours through the darkness, until at last Thorkil steered them up a river onto a graveled shore. A wall of trees pressed close to the water's edge, and within that impenetrable forest, wolf song floated in the air. The Norsemen pitched camp and kindled bonfires, small beacons in the vastness of the winter dark. They worked hastily and in silence, obedient to Thorkil's will. Even when a low voice sounded, calling their names one by one, the men did not speak. Thorkil rose and strode to the edge of the firelight, where someone stood observing them. The watcher had the shape of a man, but he was twice a man's height. Although he stood straight, he was old: His eyes were sunk deep in shadowed sockets, his flesh was gray, his beard white.

"Hail Gudmund, guardian of mortal travelers," said Thorkil.

"Hail Thorkil, bold adventurer. How is it that your people answer me not?"

"They know little of your language, lord," Thorkil replied.

The giant Gudmund smiled a chilling smile. Then he gestured, and Thorkil nodded assent. At his command, the men rose. Rank upon rank, they followed the giant along the frozen riverbank. The river turned and coiled inland through the forest into snowfields where a great hall stood. It had the shape of the mead halls they knew, long and high, but its walls were made of ice so translucent that the flames of the torches within shone through to give the building a nimbus of light. Within were gardens glittering with frost—yet the trees in these gardens were heavy with fruit.

On long tables in the hall, a feast was spread—venison and bear and sturgeon, food fit for warriors. Women waited by the trestles with drinking horns, smiling and beckoning. The mortal warriors stared, but they shook their heads and refused the feast.

"Your food is too rich for them, Gudmund," said Thorkil. The giant smiled his cold smile again. "And my daughters?" he asked. "They are fit for kings' beds."

It was true; the women were tall and slender, pale as lilies in the palace of ice. But Gorm made a courteous gesture of refusal, and his men obeyed—all but four of them, who broke ranks and, moving as slowly as sleepwalkers, took the outstretched hands. At once, intelligence and memory and the flush of life faded from the men's faces. They sank to the ice floor, no longer men but shades in a world of shades, prisoners in a borderland at the edge of a dead world.

"You will not speak nor eat nor wed my daughters," said Gudmund. "What then will you have from me?"

And Thorkil replied. They had come so far, he said, to view the world of the dead races. They desired to see the giant Geirrod in his hall, where he sat transfixed by Thor's flaming iron bolt because he had challenged the god. They wished to see the giant's daughters whose backs had

Grim was the trail to the dead lands, as Gorm of Denmark found. Near
the end of a dreary march in bitter cold, he and his warriors passed under
the empty stare of skulls. These were sentinels, set to warn off intruders.

been broken for aiding their father. And they wished to see the dwarf-wrought treasures these giants had gathered before mortal time began. He asked for safe passage into Geirrod's land and back again.

"You have it," said Gudmund. "Greet my brother Geirrod for me." And he led the company out of the ice hall and along the river to a bridge that arched the flood, gleaming dull gold in the snow light.

On the far side of the bridge was a path that crossed ridges of drifts. Beyond the drifts, a causeway traversed a flood plain. The Danes halted on the causeway, blinking at what they saw. Here was a place of horror, not meant for mortal eyes. The ground moved, belching and gulping; long threads of foul vapor curled in the air. Stakes stood along the route, each topped by a blackened human head—the relics of earlier explorers, it seemed. In the distance, a mountain rose sheer from the plain, and through the mist that wreathed it, walls and houses appeared and disappeared, straggling up the treeless slope to the crumbling walls of a feasting hall.

Among those houses the adventurers marched, ascending through streets littered with filth and the torn bodies of small animals. The company did not walk alone. From shadowed alleys and courtyards, night creatures flocked toward the living warriors: men and women of the sunless land, wraiths with pallid, shredding skin who shrieked and gibbered in unknown tongues and quickly faded into the mists—illusions perhaps, or perhaps the sleepless dead.

The Danes climbed on until they reached ladders that led to the great door of the feasting hall. It stood open, swinging on its hinges, although there was no wind. Thorkil raised his hand: "Touch nothing," he said. "Nothing here belongs to men. Look only, that you may take word of this venture back to the living." Then he and the company entered the stronghold of the old giant Geirrod.

Past doorposts black with soot they walked, into a huge chamber carved in the mountain rock. The walls crawled with coiling, fat-bodied, eyeless creatures. On the floor lay bloated bodies, human in shape, but unhumanly huge; the stench they gave off took the breath away. All around, a troop of shadow beasts—some partly human, some not recognizable as beast or man—danced and wriggled and leaped, following rhythms no man could hear.

And overseeing this dead revelry from a high seat on a rock ledge was the giant Geirrod, who before the time of man had sought to murder the thunder-god. Geirrod was pinned through the belly by a bolt of iron; black bile from his wound snaked down his legs to spread over the hair of his daughters, who squirmed and lolled at his feet. Their backs were broken; their ceaselessly turning heads lay in their laps.

Pale, grim-faced, the Danes gazed fixedly at the vengeance of the ages, eternally enacted. Then Thorkil and King Gorm passed through a high archway to the hall's treasury.

The wealth of Geirrod lay in a small chamber. The air was sweet there, and the walls gave off light that shimmered on dwarfs' work—golden tankards ringed about with silver filigree, a tusk of ivory circled with gold, gem-studded armlets, a drinking horn graven with images, and a fine woven robe and silver sword belt.

The temptation was too much for men whose lives were lived by plunder. Three of them pushed forward. One touched the ivory tusk; it quivered in his hand and plunged itself through his body. His companion was slain by a golden armlet; it became a snake and drank his heart's blood. The third man picked up the graven drinking horn; it flashed in the image of a dragon for a moment and struck the trespasser down.

Then Thorkil commanded the company to leave that place: There was too much death here. But as he turned, Thorkil himself could not forbear. He put his hand to the woven mantle where it lay in a soft heap on the stone. And when he did so, all the night creatures of that place crowded into the chamber door, their long-toothed mouths opened in demon screams, their clawed hands reaching for the intruders. The very walls seemed to sob and shout and clutch at the Danes.

They fought their way out, bowmen first, followed by spearmen and swordsmen, shooting and stabbing and slashing as they went, stumbling over stinking masses of the quivering dead, dropping to the slippery streets and running through the shadow people who wailed there. They reached the causeway, raced onto the golden bridge and left behind the screaming, furious guardians of Geirrod's land.

Of all that company, only twenty men and a single ship made it home to Den-

mark. The fame of those men lived on for centuries: Gorm and Thorkil and the others who came back with them had crossed into a world of the dead, and lived to tell the tale.

Curiosity made humans courageous. Knowing that they must die, unable to believe that something so dear and vibrant as the soul should vanish into nothingness, they searched for the worlds that lay beyond the boundaries of fleshly strength, straining for glimpses of the sunless lands that served as the last of human homes. Those lands partook of eternity; in them existed the giants of creation and the old gods who had defeated the giants, and the countless generations of thronging humanity who had walked the earth in the centuries after the gods had vanished. In those lands, one might learn the secrets of future and past, for the dead, viewing all eternity, had foreknowledge as well as memory; in those lands, one might see again dear companions who had gone to dust—fathers and mothers and lovers.

And where did the shadow lands lie? Under the earth, beyond the western desert horizon, said the Egyptians. There, a mighty subterranean river ran, flowing past a series of cave mouths that led to vast chambers where human souls huddled. Those souls spent their days in darkness, but when the sun above their prison sank, the ram-headed Ra journeyed along the river in his night barque. At the prow stood the wolf-god Upuaut, the Opener of the Ways. Ra was the sungod, and he brought light to the light-

Roused from their long sleep by the touch of human hands, old demons swarmed
down upon Gorm's company, ravenous for the flesh and blood of the living.

less. As he passed by each cavern, sunshine would gleam along its walls, and the pale shades within, remembering the world they had left, would cluster at the cave mouths, holding out their hands for warmth until the light faded as the sun-god continued on his way.

Greek souls went to a misty land that lay beyond the ocean encircling the world; the Roman dead dwelled under the earth in a vast country whose gate stood beside the vapor-shrouded shore of Lake Avernus in the Campania.

For Celtic peoples, the other world lay to the west of their lands, on islands across the ocean or beyond the mist. There, fairy people lived, and also the dead.

In writing about Celts, the Byzantine historian Procopius described a people living on the northern European coast whose duty it was to ferry souls to an island called Brittia, where, he said, the dead lands lay. At a late hour, said Procopius, these people would hear a knocking on their doors and an indistinct voice calling them to work. Then they would rise willy-nilly and walk in the dark to the shore, where they would find boats waiting. No passengers could be seen in these boats, but it was clear the vessels were heavily burdened, for they were "wet by the waves to the edge of the planks and the oarlocks, having not so much as one finger's breadth above the water." The coastal people would row their spectral cargo through the night to Brittia's shore and hear from it a voice calling names. Then the boats would lighten and rise in the water, and the living ferrymen, relieved of their ghostly passengers, would row home again.

It was a strange story Procopius told, peculiar perhaps to one Celtic tribe. Elsewhere, the dead made the journey alone, and all the aid the living could give was to provide a means of transportation, rather than actual conveyance. The Vikings, for example, buried their leaders with carts and horses and sometimes even ships.

The Norse dead inhabited a range of lands. Some said the dead had nine worlds within the earth in which to exist; some believed that they dwelled, as did Geirrod, in the farthest north; and some held that they lived on in their great howes, or funeral barrows, clustered on the plains and islands of Scandinavia. Guarded by ghost fires that flickered around the tombs, restless with whisperings and howlings, these burial fields were shunned by the living. The dead, it was thought, were fierce and jealous of the quick.

Still, these dead lands could be approached. Even as the Greek Aeneas dared the descent to the underworld to gain the knowledge and the blessing of his father and to learn all that was past or passing or to come, Vikings braved the grave mounds to seek aid from their ancestors.

In fact, tales of dying parents who promised their children protection after death — and spoke kindly to those children from their graves — were not uncommon once. Such a story was told of the Icelandic warrior Svipdag. A lord among his fellows, whose name meant "He Whose Countenance Shines Like the Day," Svipdag aroused the enmity of his stepmother. She devised a terrible test for him, placing him under oath to seek a bride in the realm where giants and elder gods still held sway.

It was a quest that meant almost certain death for even the bravest of men. The warriors of the North had not forgotten the toll taken among King Gorm's three hundred fighters in the giants' lands. Before he set out, therefore, Svipdag did as his own dead mother had told him before she died: He walked alone across the barren heath where she lay buried among the flames of the grave fires and the shifting shadows of the barrow wights, and he called upon his mother to awake, naming her name, which was Gróa.

From a mound of earth and stone a voice answered, reedy above the moaning of the wind: "What ails the son to call his mother, who has left the world of the living?"

Svipdag told what his quest must be; he asked for spells to speed his way. And Gróa, gifted with the wisdom of the dead, gave him nine charms of the ages as shield and shelter. The first charm was a kind of blessing meant to guard him. The second consisted of songs to cloak him from enemy magic that might sap his will. The third charm was a shield against rivers that would rise from the earth; this charm would cause the waters to sink back into the depths. A charm on hidden enemies' hearts was the fourth; it kept the enemies from attacking. Fifth and sixth were words to loosen fetters laid upon Svipdag and to calm wild seas that he must cross. Seventh was a charm against searing frost; eighth was a defense against night spells sent across misty moors. And last was a charm

that gave Svipdag skill in word wars, for the old ones he must face were wise and their very speech a danger.

And when Svipdag headed north toward the realm of the old ones, rivers parted before him and tempests were quelled. When the dark closed in, a flame danced in his path to light his way. In solitude, he crossed haunted moors and lightless forests; even the darkest seas let him pass.

So he came at last to the castle of the bride he sought, set in high snowfields, surrounded by ramparts of wood and a wall of fire, guarded by hellhounds and by an ancient giant. With no more than words, Svipdag fought the old one, proving his worth by wit: He battled with questions that the giant must answer. He learned that gods had built the hall and cast the fire about its walls. He spoke of the maiden hidden within; this maiden, it seemed, had gods' blood. Her name was Mengloth, meaning "Glad in Her Necklace," as if she were descended from Freya, the goddess of love, whose necklace, Brisingamen, was as bright as the sun sinking into the sea.

And at the end of the riddling, Svipdag learned his fate: Mengloth was destined for the mortal man wise enough to win her, and that man was he himself. So the giant surrendered the bride without a fight. Svipdag took her away into his own world in safety, all because of the sheltering spells of his dead mother.

Although magic was a gift of the dead, it was not primarily for magic that the living faced the terrors of their realms. Of the

From the dead, the living sometimes won aid that averted their own demise.
So it was with Svipdag, who approached his mother's grave in Iceland
and received weapons and charms that would guard him on a bride quest.

tales of ventures into the underworld, the saddest are told of lovers who sought to defy death and bring their lost companions back into the sun.

The gods themselves attempted this. One was the Mesopotamian goddess Ishtar, worshipped in Uruk, in Ninevah and in Akkad. She was the deity of love and fertility, the great mother, the divine seductress, the incarnation of the planet Dilbat, which later generations knew as Venus. Her consort was Tammuz, god of growing things and of the harvest, who died and descended to the underworld.

Stricken with grief, Ishtar followed Tammuz down into the dark place the Babylonians called the Land of No Return, the seven-gated world of the dead. It was lightless there, wrote the scribes; the dead were clothed in feathers and fed on dust and clay.

To make her way to the center of that world, Ishtar had to complete a ritual undressing. At the first stone gate she removed her starry crown; at the second, the jewels from her ears; at the third, her royal necklaces; at the fourth, her breastplate; at the fifth, her glittering belt; at the sixth, the bracelets from her arms and feet; and at the seventh, the robe she wore. When she finally reached the throne of Ereshkigal—her sister, and the queen of death as Ishtar was the queen of life—she was as naked as a child, and as helpless. She begged Ereshkigal for the resurrection of her lover. But the death queen saw herself ascendant. She made Ishtar a prisoner, tortured with disease and pain.

The whole living earth mourned Ishtar. In the reed marshes of Babylonia, the water birds died. On the great plains, the wheat and barley ceased to grow. The hot sun beat down on the cities, cracking bricks and baking the dusty streets. No animals coupled. Men and women ceased to love, and no children were born.

The old gods of wisdom, seeing the earth thus sterile and steeped in death, sent a spell to save the goddess. It was carried on the lips of a messenger who would be her substitute as prisoner, a messenger suited to the realm of dust and clay. The creature the god Ea sent was a eunuch. The substitution was accepted, and Ishtar went free again, back up the long road through the seven gates.

She brought Tammuz back to the world, it seems, for after her return, the earth bloomed again, green shoots pushing up through the cracked clay, and the beasts coupled and brought forth young once more. But every midsummer after that, as if to appease the powers of the dead, the people of Babylonia mourned Tammuz's dying with wailing flutes and hymns that likened him to the quickly fading flowers. And every year he faded again for a time, abandoning the earth during the six sterile months of winter.

Such was the power of the underworld: Death ruled all, and even the greatest gods were powerless against it. Life flourished, the worshippers of Tammuz said, only at the whim of death.

As it was in Babylonia, so it was in the North at the dawn of time. In that era, said the Norsemen, before humankind walked the earth, before the giants—first of crea-

In the realm of giants, a rampart of fire barred the fortress of Svipdag's bride. With the help of his dead mother, the young man breached the barrier to find the maiden he sought.

tures – were defeated and imprisoned in their own dead lands by the gods they had engendered, the Northern deities Thor and Odin and all the company of heaven ruled the upper air from palaces in the clouds. They had a bridge of rainbow that descended to Midgard, the middle earth – a place destined for humanity (although the gods could go there when they chose). Below middle earth lay the nine subterranean lands of Niflheim, or "Mist World" – the domain of the goddess Hel and abode of the dead. Hel's power was absolute; even the gods feared to tread her cold soil. Even Odin, the All-Father, was no more than a supplicant in Hel's world, as the story of Balder shows.

Balder, whose name meant "the Shining One," was the son of Odin and the most beloved of the gods. So precious was his life that all the spirits of earth and sky – from the waves in the sea to the trees in the forest – swore before the gods not to harm him. Only the mistletoe, lately created and apparently harmless, was exempt from the oath. Discovering this, the god Loki, slanderer and deceiver and hater of joy, persuaded a blind god to fling a bough at Balder in jest. When the wood pierced Balder's skin, the shining god fell.

Then all heaven – gods and giants, elves and dwarfs – mourned Balder and laid his body in a ship, setting it aflame so that it might vanish in the sea while his soul made its way to the underworld.

In his grief, said the chroniclers, Odin could not rest: He sent his son Hermod,

Balder's brother, to the underworld to plead with the goddess for Balder's life.

Mounted on Odin's own horse Sleipnir, the eight-legged, Hermod made the journey down the rainbow bridge and through the valleys of middle earth. For nine nights he rode, and at last he came to a cold river called Gjoll. This was the river that bordered the underworld. It was spanned by a bridge that was roofed and thatched with gold; at the bridge's gate stood a guardian, the icy maiden Modgud.

"Why do you ride the Hel-way, stranger? You have not the look of the dead," Modgud called.

"I ride in search of Balder the Shining One and of the goddess who has him in her care."

"Balder has passed by," said the maiden. "Cross into Niflheim, then. Ride north, and down."

So Hermod traveled the track that led to the halls of Hel. When he reached the towering throne hall of the goddess, he found his brother standing there – Balder, the newly dead, bringing greeting from the lands of the living.

The goddess herself looked down from her high seat. Half her face was a woman's shape, with the bright eye of a woman and the curving lip; but the other half was blank and livid, unliving and unborn.

"A supplicant," she said when she saw Hermod, and she laughed.

Then Hermod begged for Balder's resurrection. All sky and earth, he said, mourned the death of the god.

"Is it so? Then let the whole earth weep; let every thing shed tears for Balder and I will release him from my realm." It was all

In Mesopotamia, people told how the goddess Ishtar journeyed to the underworld in search of her lover. To the guardians of that realm, she gave her power that she might be reunited with the dead god Tammuz.

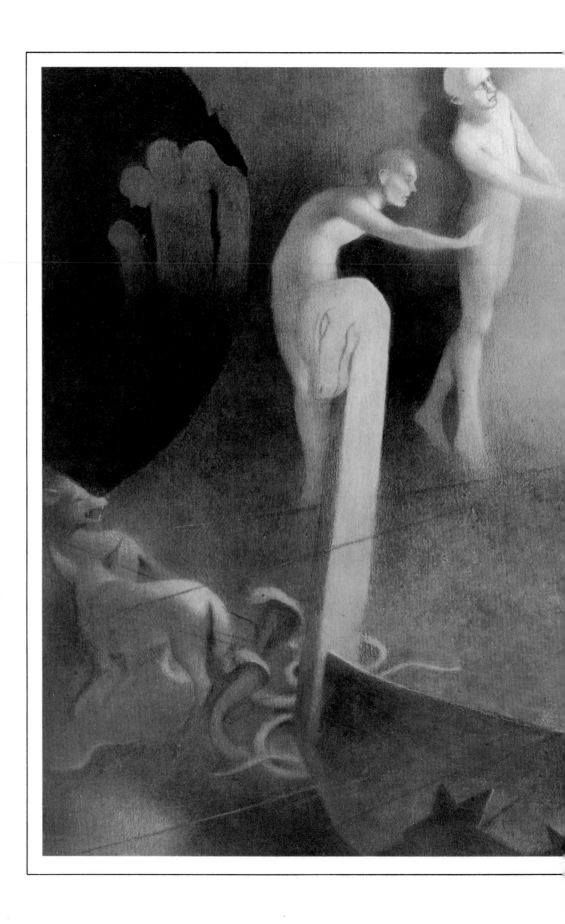

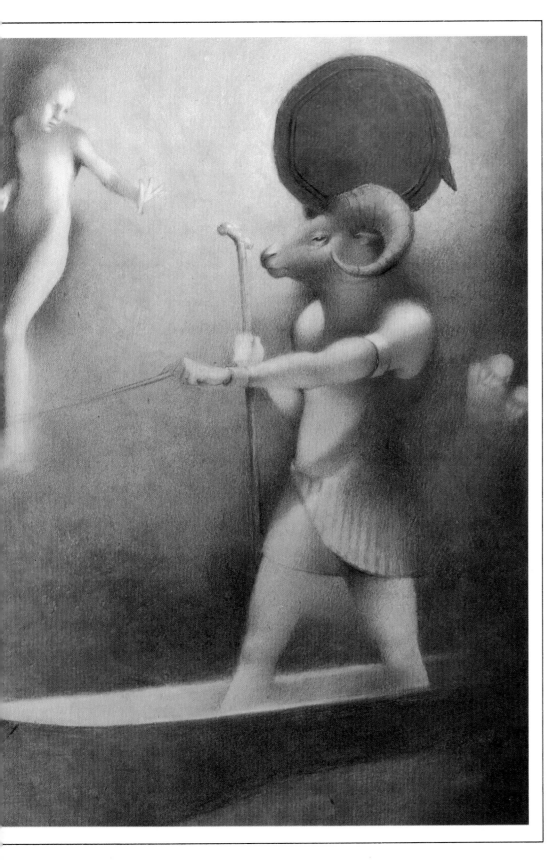

Worlds of the dead lay hidden everywhere. Under the deserts of Egypt, along a dark
river, the souls of the departed lived in gloomy caverns—brightened only for an instant
each night, when the sun-god Ra passed by on a barque towed by jackals and cobras.

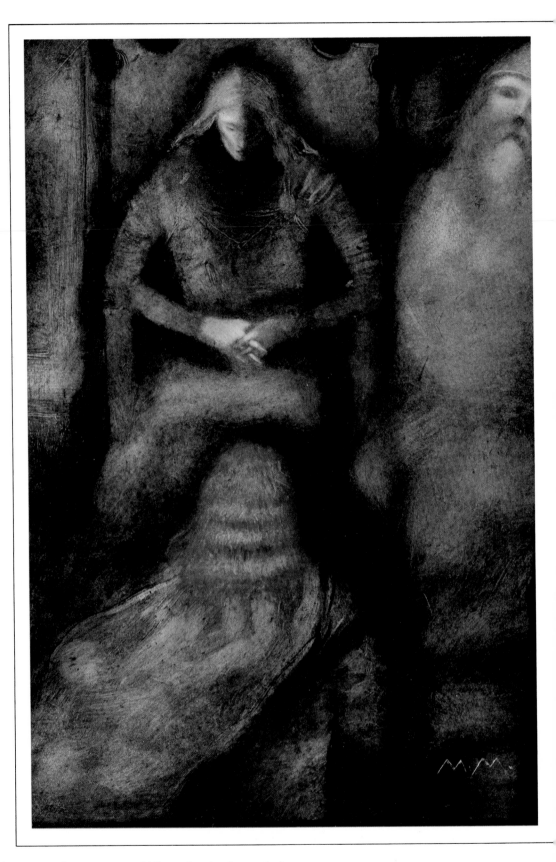

Norsemen sang of Balder, heaven's favorite son. When death claimed the
shining god, his brother traveled to the underworld and—speaking for a
grief-racked cosmos—begged the ruler of that realm for Balder's return.

the reply Hermod could take to the gods.

And at the gods' command, everything of earth and sky wept for Balder. The clouds poured rain; the leaves of the trees shed dew; droplets of tears appeared on the surfaces of stones. Only one living creature did not weep at the god's command. This was a raddled giantess wheezing sullenly in a cave. "Let Hel hold what she has," said the crone, who was Loki the murderer in another shape.

So Hel kept what she had, despite the pleading of the world.

The tales were almost always the same, whether those who dared the underworld were gods or men and women. In the end, it seemed, no one had the strength to overcome the rulers of the dark, not even Orpheus, the Greek poet and singer, whose music supposedly could call the dead back from the underworld. He ventured there to find the shade of his wife, Eurydice, and with his singing, he managed to lure her onto the cavern path that led into his own world. Indeed, he might have had her for his own again, but he paused in his singing and looked back to see if she followed, even though the gods had warned him not to gaze upon the face of one still in death's power. And when Orpheus looked, Eurydice turned and went back into the dark, leaving him forever bereft.

Of all the stories of those who pursued their loved ones, only one offered hope to the venturers. It was a small tale, buried in the chronicles of a medieval monk. The hero was not named, and was described only as a brave man and a loving one.

The account concerns a knight of Less Britain, which was the old name for Brittany. When his wife died, he buried her according to the proper rites and observed the proper mourning. But after his mourning time was over, he could not rid himself of memory or grief. He set out alone, riding east across the hills and forests. His journey took him through high mountains, along rivers and, finally, to a land of rocks and desert. In that land, on a night of a crescent moon, he found a valley crowded with pale, white-robed women. They drifted to and fro, shadows in a shadow land, making no sound on the soft sand. He rode toward them, and although no one looked at him, the throng parted so that his horse might pass.

Then dark eyes met his: His wife walked here. Without fear, without a moment's thought, he dismounted and seized her around the waist. She did not vanish, nor did she struggle. He lifted her to his horse and fled the way he had come, carrying his wife before him.

Having snatched her away from the dead world, said the chroniclers, he lived with her for many years, in a union "as pleasant and as open to the day as the first had been and had children by her, whose descendants are numerous and are called the sons of the dead mother."

His story was unique, if it can be believed at all. But there are many tales of rejoining lost loved ones in another way — by following them to the land of the dead and remaining there.

In some countries, to do so was the mark of honor and the proof of love. In lands from India to the shores of the North

No less than gods, men and women sought lost loves in the world beyond the grave. Most such efforts were in vain, but the devotion of a Breton knight was rewarded: He found his wife in a valley of shadows and drew her back into the light.

Sea, it was once the custom for wives to sacrifice themselves after the deaths of their husbands, so as to lie in their arms eternally. And Norsemen told of warrior-kings who, in the wake of battle, loaded warships with the dead and joined their comrades. It was said, for example, that a sea-king named Haki, himself badly wounded in battle, took the steering oar of such a ship, ordered the vessel set aflame and died in a great blaze upon the water, among his fallen companions. There were stories, too, of kings who, as death neared, chose to go alive into their grave mounds, followed by warriors who refused to desert their leader.

Those chiefs went into the dead world richly supplied, for the Northmen took care that their lords should exist in comfort in their dark tombs. Sometimes entire ships were buried, with the chief occupying a carved stool in the stern, to brood over the small world he now commanded. The chief's horse would be buried with him, still adorned with its trappings of silver and gold; his hunting dogs and his hawks would be laid at his feet. He would have his weapons – his sword in its sheath, his helmet of bronze, gold and silver, his chain mail, his battle-axes and his spears. His jewels would be with him, too – his golden buckle and ornaments. And he would have treasure – bowls of silver, ivory drinking horns, vessels of bronze and bags of golden coins. Nor would there be any shortage of provisions: In the holds of the funeral ship were stored chests full of grain and apples and the carcasses of sheep, cattle and pigs.

In royal splendor the chief would sit, sometimes with slaves for companions, sometimes with his wife, sometimes with his warriors. Deprived of the light of the living world, this company nevertheless had its pleasures, and some of them were content with that. They stayed quiet in the burying fields, having no dealings with the world they had left behind.

Some chiefs, however, were angry in death. Alien now to their own kind, their decomposing bodies grew in strength and fury, until they turned into the bloodthirsty creatures known as *draugar*. When this happened, the ghost fires burned bright around the barrows in the burying fields, and prudent people stayed away.

But not everyone was prudent. Though fields of the dead were dangerous, they also held treasure, and many a robber tried to desecrate the royal graves. It was robbers – albeit warriors after plunder – who chronicled the tale of Asvith and Asmund.

Those two were the sons of petty Norwegian Kings. They lived as foster brothers in the province of Vik, near a winding glacier in the western part of Norway. They learned the arts of war together, sailed together in their youth, and swore blood brotherhood. As proof of their mutual devotion, they vowed that if one should die, the other would join him, living, in the funeral barrow. It was the most serious of oaths, and it was soon fulfilled. Before he could claim his father's lands, before he could father sons to inherit them, Asvith died of a wasting illness.

Bereft, Asmund walked dully through

the days that followed, while his foster brother lay in his father's hall, white and motionless, surrounded by torches and companioned by those who watched corpses after death. Asmund waited while the women wove the grave garments and dressed his brother, while they buckled on his mail, while they draped his cloak over his shoulders and pinned it with brooches of garnet. And when they carried the body up the rocky slope of the mountain where the people buried their dead, Asmund said nothing. He walked behind, leading Asvith's horse and hunting dogs. Asmund himself sacrificed the horse and let the blood from its throat pour to the ground, a libation to those below. He speared the yelping dogs.

Then he waited as the stones were rolled aside from the burial mound and the sacrifices were lowered in. He watched while his brother's body was set on its fine carved chair. And at the last, Asmund followed, climbing down into the barrow. His companions understood; there was no wailing. They lowered in salt meat and bread for him. Then they began to fill in the entrance to the tomb with rocks and earth, hiding the gray sky where the snow was already blowing.

In the darkness, amid the reek of the slaughtered animals and the faint smell of his brother's corpse, Asmund waited for his own death. He could hear the sounds of the final chanting outside the barrow. Then the voices faded, and a deep silence found itself in the place of the dead. But the silence did not last for long.

A rustling sounded in the darkness — some earth creatures perhaps, burrowing into dead man's territory. It stopped, then it sounded again, and this time it was accompanied by the clink of mail and the scratching of nails on stone. Asmund listened intently.

"I hunger," said a guttural voice. It was his brother who spoke, rolling words indistinctly over the swollen tongue of the dead. Asmund made no reply. The clinking and the shuffling increased. The thing that had been his brother was moving now, running its dead hands around the cavern floor, searching, no doubt for food. It growled. Then Asmund heard the sharp clicking of the horse's bridle, the tearing of its flesh and the cracking of its bones as the *draugr* Asvith sought the marrow. The creature fed for hours, while Asmund sat rigid, his back braced against the cold stones of the grave wall. Then, apparently, it slept.

Asmund clutched the battle-ax that had been buried with him and waited. Eventually, the creature moved again and fed, it seemed, upon the hunting dogs, and then again fell silent.

When it awakened a third time, after hours or days — in his dark and silent prison, Asmund could not tell — it began to move around the barrow chamber, feeling its way along the walls with scratching hands, stumbling over the litter of bones of the animals that had made its feast. It neared the corner where Asmund sat, and it hesitated.

"Warm blood," it mumbled. "Is there one alive here?"

And Asmund, in a voice flat with fear,

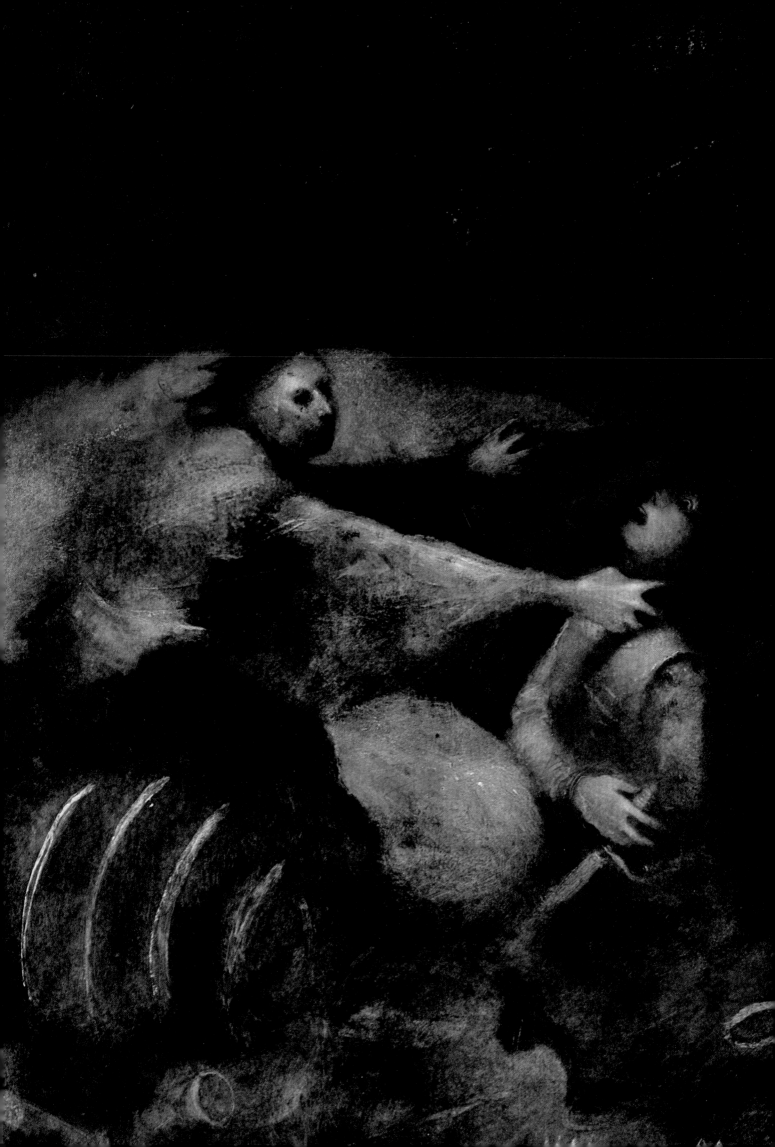

replied, "It is your brother, here as I said when I gave you my oath."

Coughing laughter echoed against the stone. "No living man may be here."

And then it struck, suddenly, as if it, unlike Asmund, could see in the dark. Iron hands wrapped around Asmund's neck; teeth tore at his shoulder and his cheek. Gasping, Asmund raised his hands, encumbered by the battle-ax. Pushing up and out, he broke the grip and reeled out of the way, toward the center of the tomb.

But the *draugr* was on him in an instant, raking claws along his cheek so that hot blood spattered on his neck. Asmund wrenched himself away, then felt pain blossom on the side of his head. Strong teeth tore into flesh: The creature was eating Asmund's ear.

Blindly, Asmund swung and swung again with the battle-ax. It met flesh, bit into bone. The *draugr* stumbled away, giving a howl that was deafening in that small chamber. Asmund followed, hacking with the ax again, and the creature that had been his brother fell heavily to the floor of the barrow. Working by feel, he cut off its head, then thrust a spear through the body, pinioning it to the ground.

After the grisly task was finished, Asmund leaned against the wall, panting and sobbing for the brother's love that could not survive the divide of dying. He closed his eyes and waited for death to claim him, too.

But death did not come. How long Asmund was there with the dead creature and the bones, he never afterward could say. Time passed without any measure except the sound of his own breathing. He grew thirsty, hungry, but he did not care. Then he heard stones rattling at the barrow entrance high above his head; gravel and earth clattered to the floor of the grave, bringing with them a rush of clear, cold air. He looked up at a patch of night sky fretted with bright stars. Then the barrow mouth darkened. Someone was being lowered into the grave, clinging to a rope. Hoarse whispers of encouragement sounded above: grave robbers.

Asmund struck when the man reached the ground. With a blow of the ax, he knocked the intruder aside and seized the rope himself. He waited a moment, then he gave it a tug and felt the pull of strong arms lifting him up into the clear air.

In a moment he had tumbled over the cave entrance and leaped to his feet to face the robbers. But they did not move toward him. They eyed him for a paralyzed instant, their eyes wide and mouths agape. Then they turned on their heels and fled.

The robbers were Swedish warriors bent on acquiring that mountain territory; they had paused on their long march to plunder the barrow. Because it was deep, they had let one of their men down into it on a rope; what came up, they thought at first, was a ghost, a warrior pale of face, scarred and hideously bloodied.

They turned at the living man's voice, however, and heard his tale and told it to their fellows. What became of Asmund they did not report. He had chosen the world of the dead; he could not stay there, being alien to it. But his history among the living ceased with his freedom. 🐍

Because of a vow, Asmund the Norseman went alive into the funeral barrow of his foster brother. He found that death had created a demon: The corpse awoke and, raging with hunger for flesh, attacked him.

Daring the Dark

When people spoke of countries that lay beyond their ken, they did not forget the world of the dead, which sheltered people like themselves who had crossed the boundaries of life. This world was fearsome, yet it was viewed with longing and curiosity, since the secrets of past and future were locked away there. Some folk dared venture into its shadows, storytellers said, and a few returned to tell what they had seen.

The Romans cited Aeneas, chieftain of Troy. "Fate's fugitive" they called him, for after the city fell to the Greeks, Aeneas stumbled from the smoking ruins, bearing his weak and aged father on his back, to embark on a life of wandering. He led the battered Trojans across the seas in search of a country where they might live. Pursued by prophetic dreams, tormented by wrathful gods whose storms took his father's life, Aeneas traveled to Thrace, to Delos, to Crete, to Carthage on the African shore. At last he landed on the Italian coast and sought out the Sibyl, prophetess of the gods: A dream had told him that she could show the way to the place where his father's ghost dwelled. The ghost, said the dream, held the key to Aeneas' future.

Wild-haired, wild-eyed, the Sibyl cried out mysteries that Aeneas could not understand. But as the dream had indicated, she agreed to lead him to the world of the dead and told how he, unlike other men, might come back again.

Thus, on a still, dark morning, Aeneas and his guide walked through a countryside of chasms and dank forest to the lake called Avernus, a round, deep water veiled with foul mist. At the lake's edge they sacrificed to the gods of hell. A cave mouth yawned. Into this cave the prophetess walked, trailing her black robes; Aeneas, following behind her, carried a branch of golden mistletoe as she had instructed him — a gift to please Persephone, Queen of Hades.

Down a stone path they trod, into the kingdom of phantoms. The road debouched into a stone cavern where a black elm stood. Each leaf of this tree, said the

Sibyl, was the ghost of an unful-
filled dream. And around the elm's
trunk a hissing crew of monsters circled: horse-bodied Centaurs, black-
winged Harpies, snake-haired
beasts. Aeneas drew his sword. The
Sibyl shook her head; these creatures, she said, were merely thin
lives, bodiless, having only the sem-
blance of shape. She led him safely
through the throngs to the banks of
the Styx, Hades' border river, where
a crowd of shades stirred and sighed,
thick as autumn leaves on the forest floor. They stretched beseeching
arms to an old and squalid man
whose small boat bobbed at the water's edge. He was Charon, ferryman
of the dead. Some shades he took
across the water, but the spirits of
those who had not received proper
burial he left to wander on the riverbank, restless and hopeless. Among
them were some of Aeneas' comrades
in battle and some who had sailed
with him on his long voyage. He saw
the poor souls and wept.

But he went forward with the Sibyl to the water's edge, and when the
ferryman, having seen the golden
bough, signaled acceptance, they
stepped onto the boat. Its planks
creaked and strained with the weight
of the living body, but it bore the
Sibyl and the Trojan to the far bank.
Past three-headed Cerberus, dog
guardian of hell, they walked into
the fields of mourning.

The fields were cloud-shrouded; mist curled and drifted around the branches of myrtle trees, and among the trees could be seen pale, drifting shapes, now visible and now not, always weeping, for these were the souls of those who had chosen death over life. In their midst was a beautiful woman, crowned and robed. Aeneas recognized her. She was Dido, Queen of Carthage, whom he had left behind. Thus he learned that she had killed herself for grief. He called to her; the poor shade gazed at him but made no reply.

They passed through the grove into a borderland where famous warriors walked. Among them Aeneas saw former companions and old enemies; Greeks and Trojans mingled there, still pierced and bloodied with their wounds. Aeneas hesitated, calling to the men he had loved and fought with, and they answered him.

But the Sibyl, anxious, urged him
onward, toward the center of that
world, where the road divided.

At the end of the left-hand road,
said the Sibyl, a fiery river rolled;
behind it rose a columned fortress
flanked by an iron tower where Tisi-
phone the Fury, gobbling and snarling, flicked a writhing whip. This
was Tartarus, the pit of Hades, and
indeed the screams and groans that
issued from the great gates suggested
the horrors that lay within.

Behind those gates of adamant,
the Sibyl explained, was a cavern
that incarcerated those who had of-
fended the gods. In the depths, the
Titans, first beings, fathers and enemies of the gods, were chained.

And in the pit were dead mortals, enduring eternal punishment for wrongs they had done in life. Some of their transgressions had been trivial, considering the price those people paid: Sisyphus, the Greek who dared to tell a river god that Zeus had abducted his daughter, forever pushed a boulder up a hill; whenever he reached the summit, it rolled back down over him and his work began again. Other offenses were terrible: In a dank pool stood Tantalus, a man who, in his fury at the heavens, had killed his own son and served the flesh to the gods. His punishment was eternal thirst: He could not bend his head to drink the waters that bubbled at his chin; he could not stretch his neck to reach the fruit that dangled above his head; and he could not achieve oblivion from the pain of his mortal body.

After the Sibyl had spoken
these things, she took the right-hand
road. It led to a gate, where she and
Aeneas left their offering for the
Queen of Hades. And when they
had done so and had passed the gate,
they arrived in a land of meadows
and green valleys, lit by its own sun,
laced with sparkling streams. These
were the fields of the blessed, said
the Sibyl. Good souls played here,
reliving life's sweet pleasures, freed
from life's cares. The air was sweet
and filled with music.

Among them Aeneas found Anchises, his father, almost transparent
now, but thoughtful and calm. The
old man regarded him gravely and
blessed his loyalty. Then Anchises
told Aeneas how he would found
the Roman Empire and sire that en-

pire's rulers. He showed Aeneas pale wisps of beings, souls gathered on a riverbank. This was the river Lethe; those whose souls were pure bathed in it, and its waters cleansed their memories of former lives. Afterward they would return to earth in newborn babies' bodies to live once again under the sky.

Then Aeneas sought to embrace his father. No embrace was possible, however; although the mortal eyes saw the old man, the mortal arms met in the air.

And the Sibyl summoned him: Their time of safety was passing. They could stay no longer than one day in the underworld, and that day was almost done.

Anchises showed them the way, through an ivory gate of dreams into the world of the living. Aeneas passed the portal. He returned to his company and to his adventures, and as his father had foretold, he settled in Italy to found the city that would be Rome, that crucible of blood and glory. Or so the Romans said when they spoke of their great past: The man who was their ancestor learned his destiny and his duty to the living in the world of the dead.

Chapter Three

A Parting of Worlds

Strangers were not unusual in the villages of East Anglia when England was young. The footpaths lacing the villagers' fields and pastures led a steady stream of brown-cloaked pilgrims to the great Benedictine abbey at Bury, where lay the tomb of Edmund, last of the ancient East Anglian kings, who had been martyred by Vikings centuries before. And soldiers of the various factions then quarreling over the English throne frequently drifted through, as well as pack-laden refugees from the west of the country, where the worst fighting was.

The farmers and shepherds, tending to their plows and the fat flocks that made them famous in the wool trade, paid most of the strangers little heed. But the coming of two children caused whisperings among the farmfolk and the millers at their wheels and the alewives in their cottages. Even the abbey monks took note of them, recording their story in words that were both pious and amazed.

The tale began with a shepherd who was whiling away a summer's afternoon on a hillside near the parish of St. Mary's, about five miles from Bury St. Edmunds. He sat in the shade of an oak copse, surrounded by his sheep. In the valley below the hill, the men and boys of the village were busy at the haying, and the shepherd could hear faint shouts or laughter from time to time. But the air among the trees was mostly quiet, except for the buzzing of flies around the sheep and the chirping of crickets.

Then the sheep flicked their ears inquiringly as a soft cry broke the peace. It was followed by a high-pitched, frantic whispering. After a few moments, when the whispering did not cease, the shepherd rose to his feet with a grunt. He ambled off through the trees in the direction of the sound.

The whispering came from an abandoned wolf-pit higher up the hill—a bowl of hard, red earth, rimmed with brambles, where wolves that threatened the town

once were thrown and left to die. The place was thought to be haunted. Reaching the edge of the pit, the shepherd stared down in astonishment.

Huddled at the bottom were a boy and a girl. Except for their fragile slenderness, they had the shapes of any children in the shepherd's hamlet. But they were clothed in leaves and flowers, and their flesh, more translucent than a human child's, was the delicate green of the young willows that bent by the banks of the Ouse in spring. Moreover, the tendrils of hair that curled around their faces were as green as the river reeds.

The shepherd made the gesture that turned evil aside: Green was the color of Faerie. Some said it was the color signifying death. But these children did not seem threatening; indeed, they were more frightened than he. They gazed up at the shepherd, hands clasped, motionless as cornered animals.

They were pitiful. He leaned toward them, resting his hands upon his knees, and said, as gently as he could, "Who are you? Who is your father?"

At his tone, the girl gave a sudden smile. She poured out a stream of syllables in a peculiar lilting cadence. None of it made sense to the man. He shook his head helplessly. Then he made the gestures for drinking and eating. This was successful: Both children nodded, and they climbed out of the pit to him.

With a whistle that made the children flinch, the shepherd set his dog to mind the sheep and led his charges down the hillside to the fields. They followed docilely enough, although they blinked and shook their heads when they emerged into the full sunlight, chattering to each other in their fluting voices. And when the three of them reached the fields, the children shrank toward the shepherd, taking his big hands in their small cool ones. The haymakers dropped their scythes and rakes as the trio approached. Tall, red-faced, sweating men, they clustered around the green children, pointing and poking and asking questions in voices that were loud with excitement.

Angered, the shepherd pulled the children away from the crowd: He was a kindly man. "Let them be. I am taking them to the master," he said. "He knows foreign tongues." Then, leaving the fields behind, he led the children to the manor house of his lord, a knight called Richard de Calne.

In the knight's timbered hall, the air was cooler, and the drooping children seemed to revive. Sir Richard heard the shepherd's tale; he sat the children on a bench and summoned his wife from her stillroom. Neither knight nor lady, however, could elicit a comprehensible word from them. The boy simply stared at the floor, slow, sea green tears rolling down his cheeks. The girl spoke, but her words told them nothing.

After watching the scene for some moments, the shepherd cleared his throat and said, "Master, these are hungry young ones." Sir Richard paused in his patient questioning. He nodded, and his lady brought hard bread and cheese into the hall. The children sniffed at it and shook their heads; this, it seemed, was not food they could eat. They refused fresh meat. They refused apples.

When the lady offered a handful of broad beans still green on their stalks, however, both children brightened. They watched while the lady ran her thumbnail along the pods, popping out the beans. These the children ate, with every appearance of pleasure.

"Are they dead folk, then?" asked the shepherd as he watched. Sir Richard and his lady understood the meaning of the question. The lore surrounding beans was ancient and — although cloudy and contradictory — frightening. The Egyptians thought beans sacred and would not eat them. The Romans believed that ghosts threw beans at houses to bring bad luck to those who lived within; in order to placate the ghosts, they threw beans on graves. Some north-country British thought that each bean housed a dead soul; others held that beans were the food of the dead.

"They are harmless," said Sir Richard. "We will care for them and make them into Christian souls." Then he gave the shepherd a farthing for his trouble and sent the man on his way.

For some months, the shepherd saw nothing of the children. When summer had deepened into autumn and cold rains began, he brought his flock down into pens in the valley near the manor. He heard talk of the children then, from grooms and servants. The girl had learned English, the gossips reported. The monks had come to speak with her. They did not mention the boy; evidently, no one had glimpsed him since the day he arrived.

The shepherd made no comment; he merely kept his eyes open. And eventually, on a clear, cold afternoon in November, when a rosy sunset streaked across the blue of the sky and the evening star appeared, the green girl sought him out where his sheep were penned. He saw her approach from a distance, flitting across the meadows that lay near the manor house, and he waited.

She had changed. She wore the woolen gown and cloak of any human child. As she drew close, the shepherd perceived that the leafy color had faded from her flesh and hair. Although her face was pale, it now glowed in the autumn air; her hair was like silver gilt.

"Why, shepherd, I have found you," she said, and smiled at him.

"How goes it with you, child?"

She was well, she replied. She ate the food of this world now and so took on its color; she could speak with her fellows; she served in Sir Richard's household. As she spoke, she moved about, restless as a butterfly, touching the shepherd's cloak, the fence that restrained his sheep, the backs of the sheep themselves.

"And the boy?"

"He is dying," said the child. "He lies on his bed, a green branch all twisted, for he cannot eat the food here. He belongs in our land, not this one."

When the shepherd asked where her own land was, she replied vaguely, as if the memories were fading from her mind. She and her brother had lived in a world without a sun, a place whose daylight was like the twilight here on earth. It was a pretty world, rich in crops and animals. She and her brother had left it one day when they were minding their flocks.

"You have sheep there, like these?" asked the shepherd.

"Not sheep," she answered. "Beasts you would not know." But she could not describe them.

On the day they had left their world, she said, they had discovered a cave leading into a mountainside; from the darkness within came faintly chiming bells, so clear and sweet that the children were charmed. They left their flocks and entered into the cave mouth. Drawn onward by the bells, they walked through a twisting tunnel, following its turns until they saw light ahead. The music of the bells grew louder. They walked through an arch and found themselves in the clay pit. At that instant, the chiming of the bells ceased. Frightened by the blinding light, they turned for home. But the portal in the earth had closed. Not even a seam showed in the dust of the pit. The next thing the girl could tell of the venture was the sight of the shepherd himself, staring down at them from the edge of the pit.

The girl and the shepherd talked on for a little while; then she left to return to the warmth of the manor house.

He did not speak with her after that. In the spring, he heard that the boy had died, growing more and more like a crumpled leaf as he failed. The girl continued in the service of Sir Richard. She grew into a woman and, like any country wom-an, married. But she remained a flighty, rather thoughtless creature, mercurial in her ways. The countryfolk, no doubt having seen how she haunted the green shade of the forests, how she loved to dally among the reeds of the riverbanks and linger in the meadows at twilight, murmured that she was loose and wanton. It was the only way they had, perhaps, to describe a being so like them yet so alien.

Who were the green children, and where was their land? The chroniclers did not know: By the time the fairy girl had English enough to tell them her history, she had absorbed so much of humanity that her memory was clouded. The monks who recorded her venture could only say that a gateway between worlds once had opened, letting two wanderers through, and then had closed again.

As mysterious as the children were, however, their curious exile showed in miniature the rules that governed journeys between the world of mortals and the older lands that lay just out of human view. No matter how much delight men and women took in fairy people, no matter how great the loves that grew between them, their worlds belonged to different ages, the one just born, the other fading into its death. No one could travel with total freedom between the realms. In the end, a choice had to be made by human and fairy alike: to stay with one's own kind or to vanish into the life of another era.

In the earliest times of humanity's rule, when movement was still common between the mortal world and that of Faerie, wise folk of both races knew that a breach was approaching. Its signs were evident in

With its different rhythms and rules, the mortal world sapped the strength
of those whose home was Faerie. Once, a green child from an enchanted land was
trapped among humankind. He faded to a wraith and finally breathed no more.

As if to show that different worlds must be forever divided, Manannan,
Ireland's sea-god, passed a cloak of enchantment between the hero Cuchulain
and the fairy woman Fand, erasing from each the memory of the other.

the tale of the Irish hero Cuchulain, the Red Branch Knight, who had himself been trained for war in the other world and regularly crossed its borders. It happened once that Cuchulain was enticed away from his own country and from Emer, his wife. He fought side by side with the fairy people in a battle; his reward was the love of a Princess named Fand, whose beauty was clearer, the storytellers said, than a tear that glistened in an eye.

Cuchulain stayed with Fand for a month and it seemed to him that no woman — not even his young wife, Emer — could match her. But his honor demanded that he return to his own people. When he took his leave of the fairy, however, she said, "In whatever place you tell me to go and meet you, I will go there."

This was love and courage, to leave her own kind and follow him. Cuchulain made a trysting place for them — by a yew tree that grew at Baile's Strand, a wave-washed shingle on the shores of the Irish Sea — and there Fand joined him on the day he had determined.

They had little pleasure on that day. Cuchulain had only time to take the fairy into his chariot. Then she cried out: A troop was approaching. It was a company of women, armored in gold breastplates and armed with long green knives. The leader was Emer.

"Do not fear these women, Fand," Cuchulain said. "My spear will guard you."

His mortal wife drew her own chariot beside his. Unmoved, he listened as she reproached him for the dishonor his infidelity had brought upon her. He could not remain unmoved, however, when proud Emer dropped the long knife she held and wept, begging him to return to her. In the silence that followed her weeping, Cuchulain made his choice: "You are pleasing to me, wife," he said, "and will please me as long as I live."

It was said that Fand left then, lamenting her lot to be cast off by the hero. Manannan the sea-god appeared to her on the water and led her away from the mortals.

*C*uchulain withdrew into grief, said the storytellers, loving two women and lacking one of them. He wandered, until the wise men of his tribe gave him a wine to induce forgetfulness. They poured this for Cuchulain and also for Emer, so she might not remember her grief and jealousy. And the sea-god made sure that the love between mortal and fairy could not bloom again. Manannan called Cuchulain to the shore, where the water rippled on the stones. Fand was there, still beautiful, still mourning for Cuchulain. Then Manannan passed his cloak between them, so that they might forever afterward be lost to each other's sight and memory.

In eras later than Cuchulain's, those who chose a world not their own faced almost insurmountable difficulties. There were, for instance, many sad tales of men who loved and married fairy women and brought them into the world of humankind, only to lose them through their own human failing. Such marriages always were hedged with special rules: The husband must not question his wife about her life before him, or he must never strike her, or he must not look upon her at certain

times. The husbands invariably broke the rules, and their wives invariably disappeared when they did.

So the Normans told of a knight named Henno, who, one day while hunting, came upon a maiden sitting alone in a forest, a maiden so fair and loving that he took her away with him to his home and married her. She asked only to be given one day of solitude each week. The entranced Henno readily agreed to this. That period of privacy began after the saying of the morning mass, but Henno's mother noticed that the bride always left before the elevation of the Host. Alarmed, she followed her daughter-in-law to the chamber where she bathed. And she discovered that the bride was no mortal; in the shifting way of fairies, she sometimes changed her shape, and on this day she took the shape of a serpent. Appalled, mother and son summoned a priest. He sprinkled the woman with holy water, and with a cry of pain, she vanished from the mortal world.

Such unions were difficult to keep, no matter what world they were made in: However strong the love between the two beings, the tie to one's own kind remained intact. Seeking to protect themselves in their ventures to Faerie and secure their freedom to come home, humans made safeguards for themselves. It was believed that they could travel there with impunity if they did not eat the fairies' food or drink their wine or take their gold. Doing these things would sap their strength and trap them in enchantment. Perhaps the same rules applied to fairies too: The green girl, in eating human food, lost some of her fairy nature, enough for her to survive among mortals; her brother, unwilling or unable to exist on human fare, died among the strangers.

Sometimes the safeguards were effective and sometimes they were not. The ways of Faerie were capricious, and its powers ebbed and flowed.

In this vein, Norsemen cited the example of Helgi Thoreson, son of a chieftain. He was sent north with a company of his father's people to trade for furs with the hunting and trapping tribes of Finnmark. It pleased him to go: In the winter, when coastal waters froze and storms tormented the oceans, warriors could not engage in raiding, and the Norsemen grew restless, longing for adventure.

Helgi found adventure—more than he had anticipated. Somewhere in the Finnmark snowfields, he became separated from the others of his company. How this happened, the chroniclers did not say. In any case, Helgi was a hardy young man, and he rode on, past icy lakes and stands of bare-branched trees, toward a pine forest where he might find shelter.

He traveled for some hours among the tall trees, in fading light that tinted the frosted ground blue. At length he passed into a place of mist. It curled shawl-like around the trees and veiled the ground. Helgi halted, waiting for the way to clear.

Suddenly, his horse's head jerked up; the animal stamped and sidled. A soft glow appeared in the white air. Figures moved around the light, indistinguishable to him. He drew his sword.

The changeable nature of other-world folk struck fear into mortal hearts. A Norman knight's fairy bride, found shifting into serpent shape, was banished by her husband and his people.

Wandering in a wood where the way was lost, Helgi Thoreson of Norway
crossed a border he did not see, into a land he did not know. There, a Princess of
that land caught him in enchantment that dissolved all ties to his own folk.

In the next moment, however, he sheathed it, for the mist parted and revealed a wonderful sight. Scattered here and there among the trees was a company of women—beautiful women cloaked in scarlet. They seemed made of gold: Their hair shone in the winter twilight; around their necks great torques of twisted gilt gleamed, and the bridles of their horses glittered with gems.

The leader of the troop advanced a few paces and observed Helgi with steady eyes. Then she spoke in a voice like the sighing of the wind in the trees. "Hail, mortal," she said. "I am Ingeborg, daughter of Gudmund, the thousand-year King of the land called Glasisvellir. If you follow, you will find shelter."

Enchanted by Ingeborg and heedless of the peril of joining such creatures in such a place, Helgi followed the horsewomen. Ingeborg rode ahead of him, straight-backed and graceful. Only once on that ride did she turn her head to look at him, and Helgi trembled before her glance.

In time, they came to a clearing. A great tent, pitched on the snowy ground, shimmered icelike before Helgi's eyes. Within were piles of white fur and rugs of silk, such as Helgi had seen when eastern traders came to his homeland. A blazing fire filled the tent with warmth; lamplight shone on vessels of silver laid out, it seemed, for a king's feast.

Ingeborg dropped her scarlet cloak to the ground. "Stay with me, Helgi Thoreson," she said softly. He nodded, speechless, and at that moment, Ingeborg's sisters vanished. He was alone with her.

Helgi remained at the forest camp for three days. But he was the son of his father, and even in his enchantment, he did not forget his home. At last, he spoke of it. Ingeborg only smiled. As she did so, her sisters appeared one by one. They led him to his horse: Its packs were laden, one with silver and one with gold.

"The beast will find your way for you, Helgi Thoreson," said Ingeborg. Helgi mounted his horse. When he turned back to say his farewell, the tent and the women had vanished.

This much Helgi told his father when he was safe in his wooden hall once more. But he said little else of his venture. Months passed; Helgi hunted with his fellows; he sailed with them on their expeditions, but he had become a silent man, grieving for the woman of enchantment.

Helgi's father and his father's King figured in the completion of these events. The King was in his father's hall on the night of the winter solstice a year after Helgi's venture. The hearth fires burned bright; the drinking horns were passed freely around, and the singing grew louder as the hours wore on. Outside, beyond the warmth of the hall, the winds whistled.

Then the voice of the wind rose to a screaming gale. The rafters creaked; the hearth fires flickered, and the heavy hangings on the walls stirred. With a roar, the doors flew open, and a cloud of snow blew into the hall. Great hands reached from this cloud. They snatched at Helgi Thoreson and pulled him into the whiteness. Then the snow cloud settled to the floor of the hall, puddling and

The tears of his people summoned Helgi Thoreson back to his own land. But he could no longer see it; frail now and blinded by the powers of Faerie, he belonged to the Princess he had found in the wood between worlds.

steaming in the heat. Helgi had vanished.

Although his father sent search parties across the land, Helgi was not seen again until a full year had passed and the night of the solstice called him forth. He strode into his King's hall, a man fair and strong and shining with happiness, although he did not speak. Two armed companions walked beside him, bearing in their hands great drinking horns of gold. They knelt before Helgi's father and before his father's King and presented the horns to them.

Then, said the chroniclers, the King raised his hands to give the gifts a Christian blessing. When he did so, the fire and the torch-flames died with a hideous shriek, leaving the hall in darkness. In the confusion that followed, steel clanged and screams shivered on the air. Then the fire kindled of its own accord and illuminated the strained faces of the warriors in the hall. Helgi and his companions were gone. Three of the Norsemen lay dead.

After that, Helgi's father sent out no more search parties. He could not defeat the powers of the thousand-year King from the North or the enchantments of the King's daughter. But he did not cease to mourn and pray for his son's return; in his thoughts, he continually called Helgi's name, summoning him to his own world.

And because of this never-ending call across the border of the worlds, because of the strength of the father's will, Helgi reappeared again among his fellows. But he was no longer a shining warrior of the North. Instead, he was a bitter man, drawn against his will from the world he had chosen, and much changed in consequence. He had been blinded, so that he might not look upon his own kind again. He was emaciated and listless; his voice was flat and cracked, and his steps were shuffling, as if the strong soul that made him a man had gone. His father's will had defeated enchantment, but the son who returned was not the son who left. Helgi's spirit stayed, it seemed, in the world of the North.

The price of venturing between the worlds, the old tales seemed to say, was the division of the self. Those who crossed the boundaries lost definition; they became as ghosts, belonging not to one place or the other. Wherever they lived, their lives were dimmed by longing.

The yearning and restlessness were especially marked in tales concerning children born of unions between mortals and the beings of the other world. These children often had special vision and special powers. Some were kings, some great heroes. Yet all were souls divided: They were human and trod the earth like other men and women, but in their veins flowed magic, and the call of the other world rang always in their ears.

Such children were to be found in every country in the ages before the gates of magic shut, for when the issue was love and desire, boundaries between worlds were breached no less often than boundaries between human kingdoms. More of these children, however, seemed to live in the spell-haunted plains and mountains of Ireland than in any other place.

This is not surprising. The history of that emerald island set in its silver ocean was one of repeated invasions by different races, all of whom — before the advent of humankind — were gifted with magic. Of the earliest invaders, the most powerful were the Fomorians, a ferocious, seagoing tribe that sometimes appeared in mortal form and sometimes as creatures composed of hideous conjunctions of beast and human parts. The Fomorians were driven from Ireland to the remotest islands of the western seas by the Tuatha Dé Danann, a race of godlike warriors, gifted in enchantment. The Tuatha themselves disappeared — although they did not die — when human tribes grew strong in Ireland.

All of these changes took place over many centuries, and the distinctions between the races never were clear-cut. The Tuatha rulers, it was said, enhanced the power of their bloodlines through unions with Fomorians. Later, after the Tuatha had retreated to underground kingdoms and enchanted islands, they maintained their vigor by marriage with the flower of humankind: warriors and their sisters, great kings and their daughters.

In the days of Ireland's glory, when warriors of the Fianna patrolled the hills and shores for the High King, one of these unions led to the birth of the warrior Oisin. Oisin's father was Finn Mac Cumal, the Fianna's leader. His mother was a Tuatha woman who, in the guise of a deer, appeared one day while Finn was hunting. She followed Finn to his fortress on the Hill of Allen in the east of Ireland. When she was within the safety of its walls, she showed herself in her true shape — that of a beautiful woman. Finn loved her at once and kept her by him. In time, however, the woman was wrested from Finn — captured by her enemies within the Tuatha. Finn never saw her again, but after many years, he found the child she had borne him, a wild boy who had grown up in the wilderness in the care of a deer. The older man recognized this boy as his son and took him in charge, to be brought up with honor as a son of the Fianna.

Oisin grew, indeed, to be the most admired of that company. Son of the chief, he was beautiful of body and skilled in the arts that the Fianna cherished: in running and jumping, in woodsmanship, in battle with spear and with bow. He was brave, said the bards, and could "overtake a deer at its greatest speed and see a thistle thorn on the darkest night." In addition, perhaps because of his fairy blood, Oisin had the gift of poetry and song — more than any of his fellows, skilled poets all.

He hunted with his fellow warriors; he camped with them through the summers, when the Fianna lived on the land; and in the winter he sang in the halls of their strongholds. He married a woman called Eibhir of the Plaited Yellow Hair and with her had a son called Oscar, who became a great warrior in his own right.

Although he shone among the Fianna and shared the love of that fighting brotherhood, Oisin did not stay in Ireland. The story of his leaving, he himself told:

It happened one summer's morning that the warriors gathered to hunt in Munster near Loch Lein, a flat lake bordered by reeds thick with waterfowl, and by woods

*Entranced by Niam of the Golden Hair, the warrior Oisin left his kin and country. Across
the western seas from Ireland he rode, carrying the Princess back to her hidden realm.*

where deer played. In the morning, the mist rose from the lake surface; the birds sang in the trees and called among the rushes. The hunting was fine. Toward noon, when the mist had burned off and the sun had risen high, the men threw themselves on the ground in the shade of the trees. They rested and talked lazily.

Then, from the west, at the far edge of the lake, a rider appeared, moving fast. The horse was a white one, crowned, bridled and shod with gold, but it was not as golden as its rider. She was a beautiful woman, paler than the swan upon the wave, Oisin later said, with eyes as blue and clear as the dew on the grass and golden hair hung with gold rings. She rode straight to the place where the men of the Fianna lay. They rose to their feet.

"What is your name, lady, and what is your country?" Finn asked.

"Chief of the Fianna, I am Niam of the Golden Hair, and I am the daughter of the King of the Land of the Young."

She was a fairy, then—one of those whose lands lay in the ocean, far to the west. Her father was the sea-king Manannan Mac Lir.

"What has brought you from over the sea, lady?" Finn asked.

"I have given my love to your son Oisin," replied Niam of the Golden Hair. Her eyes rested for a moment on Oisin.

He walked slowly to the horse. His eyes were shining; the fairy woman's son was a stranger to his fellows already. Tears filled Finn's eyes, and he turned his head away.

"A true welcome, young Princess," Oi-sin said. "You are the shining one. It is you I choose."

When he gave this consent, Niam put a word bond on him, called a *geis* by the Irish. Such a bond could not be broken. It said that he must come away with her to the Land of the Young. There, Niam said, the trees bore fruit and leaves and flowers all at once. This was a country where death never visited, where Oisin would have a golden crown and all the weapons of the greatest warriors and all the music in the world. And there were delights beyond these, but she had not leave to tell him of them.

Then Oisin kissed his father, averting his eyes from the older man's grief-drawn face. He mounted the white horse behind Niam. Finn whispered, "You are my son whom I never shall see more."

But Oisin merely touched his heels to the horse and set off with Niam. They rode across Munster until they came to the sea. There, the horse pawed the shingle and shook its mane. It gathered itself and leaped, not into the water but onto the crest of the waves, where the foam played and the sunlight sparkled. Out over the sea, the white horse galloped, quicker than the spring wind on the backs of the mountains. Far across the plain of blue it went, until Ireland dwindled to a line on the horizon and vanished altogether.

Speeding above the water, the horse never tired. But it halted once, near the shore of a rocky island where a stone tower rose. "Will you show me your courage, husband?" Niam asked. "On that island lies a sister of my tribe, held by an old

In the Land of the Young, where the trees gave forth flower and fruit together
and time was different from mortal time, Oisin and Niam were welcomed with honor.

one, for there is none to defend her."

Oisin did that: He urged the horse to the rocks and dismounted. And while Niam held the horse offshore, prancing on the waves, Oisin met the enemy—a misshapen, naked, barely manlike creature that crawled across the stones and reared, showing its teeth and claws and spitting bile. It lunged at Oisin. The warrior feinted and slipped back, and at once it was upon him, its oily eyes gleaming as it sought his throat. Then Oisin thrust, and his sword bit into the naked belly. With a shriek, the creature toppled backward. It twitched for a moment, then seemed to fade and melt into the rock.

Niam called out; for an instant only, Oisin saw the sister of her tribe, a fairy woman freed from a Fomorian. The woman raised her hand; then she slipped by him and skipped onto the surface of the sea. She seized a curl of foam as though it were a chariot's reins, and a wave bore her away. Oisin never learned her name or how she had come to be captured. She was part of an old tale, Niam said, and now her part was played.

Through that fairy, Oisin had given proof of his valor. Afterward, Oisin and Niam rode the waves to the Land of the Young. A sea-king met them on the shore with a hundred thousand welcomes. Then, Oisin stayed in that rich land where the trees bore both fruit and flower and the birds sang bell-like harmonies. He lived in splendor with his fairy wife. Three children were born to them, two boys whom Oisin called Finn and Oscar, after his father and his son in his own world, and a girl whom he named simply "The Flow-er," for she showed her mother's beauty.

But Oisin had human blood. The never-ending procession of days and years and the quiet joys of the Land of the Young made him restless for the harder life he had known. He would stand on the seashore, gazing east, and he would speak of Finn to Niam, and tell her of his longing to see his home once again.

At last, grieving, Niam told him to take the white horse and seek out his father and his fellows and the land he yearned for. She warned him that his world would not be as he remembered, but in his eagerness he did not heed her. She warned him that if he once dismounted so that his feet touched the soil where men and women ruled, he would never again journey to the Land of the Young.

Oisin left Niam weeping on the shore, as he had once left his father. He sped off across the sea on the fairy horse.

Even the shoreline of Ireland had changed. Where it had been wild and empty, except for the forts that crowned the headlands and kept watch over the sea, it was dotted with the huts of fishing villages. Only crumbling walls showed where the great forts had been. Oisin rode on the swift horse across plains and mountains to the Hill of Allen, where his father's stronghold had stood. But no high ramparts loomed white upon the limestone hill; no bands of hunters wound down the road that led to the Leinster water-meadows. The hilltop was smooth and patched with grass; a few tumbled stones lay here and there. The rest, it seemed, had

Longing for home, Oisin left the Land of the Young. But centuries had passed: His people were gone, and when his foot touched Irish soil, the mighty warrior turned into an old man.

been taken away to build the cottages that straggled down the hillside.

Oisin rode among the cottages. The villagers were small, poorly dressed people, who inched back from the muddy track and pulled their forelocks when they saw him, Oisin the Golden, riding on the moon white horse. His hand was the size of one of their skulls. Men had shrunk while he lived in the Land of the Young, where time moved to a different measure.

He rode near a small group struggling with a boulder. They scattered, gabbling and pointing. He greeted them courteously, great lord that he was, and because he was strong and they were weak, he leaned from the saddle to push away the rock. As he leaned, the saddle girth strained and snapped. Oisin fell, and a veil of darkness descended over his eyes.

When he awoke, he found himself staring up at the sky. He was lying on the ground, and he was cold. He moved his head feebly; grit scratched beneath it. At once, hands went around his shoulders to help him to sit up. As he moved, pain shot through his stiffened joints. Head bent, he stared down at his hands. They were bony and knotted; the papery flesh was spotted with brown, and the cracked nails were thick and yellow.

Near his right ear, a voice sounded as from a distance: "How is it with you, old father?" Oisin turned his head and saw reflected in a young woman's anxious eyes the image of himself, with white hair straggling in thin wisps from a pink skull, with drooping lips and quivering cheeks.

Thus Oisin learned his fate: The brief years he lived in his mother's country had passed as centuries in his father's. Only the white horse of Niam – part of Faerie itself – had protected him from the ravages of the world's time. When his feet touched the earth walked by humans, his human blood rose ascendant and delivered him back to mortal time.

The poor countryfolk were kind to him. They heard the tale he told in his trembling voice, and in turn they recited to him the legends of the names he mentioned. They told how the Fianna had risen against the High King; how they had lost their best men at the Battle of Gabra; how those who had not died had scattered; how the fortress on the Hill of Allen had slowly crumbled in the wind and rain.

A stranger in his own land, the old warrior had nothing left but lamentation. He sang of his youth, of the sound of the blackbirds caroling on spring mornings, of the voices of the hounds as the men headed for the hunt, of the stags belling in the hills. He sang of battles and of the crows screeching in the sky above the armies. He spoke all the names of the Fianna, and he related their deeds, that they might not be forgotten.

At the last, before he died, Oisin sang his own sorrow. The reedy old voice keened on; the people remembered the words that accompanied the ancient warrior's end:

"I am a shaking tree," he sang. "My leaves are gone; I am an empty nut, a horse without a bridle; a people without a dwelling place, I Oisin, son of Finn.

"Without rising up to do bravery as we

were used, without playing as we had a mind; without swimming of our fighting men in the lake; it is long the clouds are over me tonight.

"There is no one at all in the world the way I am: It is a pity the way I am; an old man dragging stones; it is long the clouds are over me tonight.

"I am the last of the Fianna, great Oisin, son of Finn, listening to the voice of bells; it is long the clouds are over me tonight."

So Oisin described the splendors of his youth to a people who had forgotten true splendor. He was a relic of a poet's age in a prosaic world, a last whisper of a time when magic freely moved upon the earth. Oisin's lament was the sign that the age had ended.

To be sure, tales of fairy beings who found their way to the lands ruled by humankind continued to be told. But many of the tales were obscure chronicles of ephemeral encounters—the last breath of the winds that blew between the worlds.

The children of these encounters were not heroes, honored, as Oisin was, for the fairy blood that endowed them with valor and with poetry. The world of Faerie and the workings of magic came to be feared by humankind; the sons and daughters of Faerie were brushed with strangeness, and men and women viewed them with suspicion. It is no wonder that these children's parents sought to hide their ancestry. But that was not an easy task, for the children themselves were pulled toward the lands of Faerie by the blood in their veins.

The French told of such a child, who lived many centuries after Oisin had left the earth. The child's mother was a Breton Queen, a pretty woman kept in a forest palace like some precious jewel. Yet, for her husband or her people, her prettiness did not balance the fact that she was barren. After ten years of marriage, the King had no heir—a serious matter.

She walked one morning in a walled garden of the castle, where espaliered vines ornamented the stone and the walls were lined with peach and apricot trees that had been cunningly forced by grafting to flower and fruit. Because they were just outside the natural order of things, such trees, called ymp trees, sometimes provided portals to places outside nature. Perhaps the Queen knew this as she paced the garden paths, weeping for the child she did not have.

A horse whinnied softly at the open garden gate. She turned. A rider waited there, observing her. He was a tall man, young and shining of hair, crowned with a circlet of gold. "Is it a child you yearn for, lady?" he said. "Then come with me to the border of my land, and I will give you a child who will be the sun of this court."

Without a word, the Queen let this stranger take her up before him and ride out through the palace gate. They went to a lake not a league from the castle, a small lake bordered by willows and fringed by grass. In the shade of the trees, the stranger dismounted and took the Breton Queen in his arms.

Some hours later, when the light had begun to fade, the stranger said, "Now, lady, my land lies under the forest; this is its entrance. Mark it well, that you may tell

A man who never slept had fairy blood, a storyteller told the Breton
     Prince Tydorel, who was just such a man. The revelation kindled the
young Prince's heart and sent him in search of his unknown father.

it to my son when he asks." And without another word, he rode into the waters of the lake and disappeared.

The Queen never saw the stranger again. A son – not her husband's – was born to her, and she named him Tydorel. He grew up to be lean and handsome. Bred from his birth to kingship, he was smooth of speech, skilled in the courtier's arts, a fine swordsman and bruising rider. But the people looked askance at him; he lacked any quality of repose, and his disposition was as restless as his body, now bright, now cold and dark.

He never slept, so the Queen hired poets to read to him at night, and storytellers to entertain him. From time to time, she would glance into his chambers late at night. She would see Tydorel pacing swiftly up and down while the candles guttered, his companions slept and the taleteller droned quietly on.

Night after night through his youth, the Queen watched. If Tydorel knew of her vigil, he did not say, but then he rarely spoke with her as the years wore on. He seemed to be waiting for a word, and one night he had it, from a goldsmith the Queen had ordered to instruct him with accounts of his trade.

"I know no tales, young master," said the man when Tydorel asked for an amusing story, "but I know this: A man who does not sleep has no mortal for a father." Then the goldsmith folded his arms and stared at the Prince, defiantly silent.

The Queen left the corridor where she had been listening and returned to her chambers, dismissing her ladies. In moments, her son stood before her, trembling in the way he did when his quick rages were upon him.

"Did you hear?" asked Tydorel.

"I heard," answered the Queen. "The man spoke truly. Your father is a King in the land that lies under the forest."

"Why did you not tell me?"

"I wished to keep you by me," the Queen replied, and she wept.

"How shall I find the land of my father?" said Tydorel, heedless of his mother's grief. She told him.

Without another word, not even a farewell, Tydorel turned on his heel and left her. She followed, down the long corridors, past the guards, to the stables. When he rode out, she followed, but Tydorel did not spare her a glance.

Drawn by some force the Queen could not reckon, Tydorel thundered through the moonlit forest, straight to the lake that was the gateway to the world beneath the wood. As he reached its verge, the gold-crowned stranger rose from the water, arms outstretched. With a shout, Tydorel spurred the horse and plunged across the lake, his horse's hoofs striking up glittering spray. The stranger-King glanced at the Queen on the lake edge; then he raised his arms higher still. Father and son vanished into the waters.

So the son of a human mother, reared and nourished in the world of men and women, was drawn back into the land of the fairy who had fathered him. Tydorel was never seen again. The gates were closing: The people of the old world no longer had a place in the new. ⌇

Tydorel found his fairy father rising in welcome from a forest lake. The
Prince plunged into the waters and was never again seen by humankind.

The Countess of the Fountain

"Three knights of battle were in the court of Arthur," recounted the bards of Wales. "Cadwr, the Earl of Cornwall, Lancelot du Lac and Owein, the son of Urien. And this was their characteristic: that they would not retreat from battle, neither for spear, nor for arrow nor for sword." The knights had need of stubborn courage. As the tale of Owein shows, they searched for adventure in worlds not their own – worlds encircled by ancient mysteries and ruled by laws that were baffling to humankind.

Owein went seeking a certain country that he had heard about from his fellow warriors. In a summer month, he rode north from Arthur's stronghold at Caerleon. For many days he traveled through high mountains, eventually reaching a border region where uncharted forests swept into the distance as far as the eye could see. He found a castle in this borderland, as his companions had said he would, and there kindly strangers greeted him and feasted him. Finally they sent him away on a track that led into the forest's depths.

In the heart of the wood was an old god, a giant creature, dark as night. The god stood on a single leg, regarding the intruder coldly. His antlered head brushed against the tree branches. When he called, the animals of the wood streamed into the clearing, clustering in the grass at his feet and bowing their heads to the ground. In the face of such power, Owein bowed too. Then he asked the god where he might find adventure – as if this were not adventure enough.

The god's eyes crinkled with laughter at the man's presumption. But he spoke. He told Owein where he must ride and what he

would find there, and Owein left him. The knight followed a track through the forest to a sunny valley where a single tree towered, spreading enormous, sheltering branches all around. In this tree's shade stood a stone fountain. On the fountain, fastened with a silver chain, a silver bowl lay. As the god had bidden him, Owein leaned from his horse, drew water from the fountain using the silver bowl, and then poured it out.

Among the surrounding woods, thunder rolled. The sky darkened. The wind howled, and borne on its fury came a volley of hail, clattering against the shield Owein raised above his head and bouncing thick and white as stars upon the grass. Man and horse braced silently in the gale and waited.

The fury ended as suddenly as it had begun. All the leaves of the great tree had fallen; above Owein's head on the now-bare branches, bright-colored birds sang to greet the returning sun.

Owein had no time to listen to their singing, however. A warrior rushed down from the forested slope of the valley. He was the guardian of the fountain, armed all in black and mounted on a black charger, and his lance was at the ready, its tip leveled at Owein's heart.

The young man had time only to swing his horse around and lower his own lance into position before his enemy was upon him. The force of the impact broke both warriors' spears and knocked the men to the ground. After a stunned moment, they rose and drew their swords.

Back and forth under the bare branches of the tree they fought, wielding their broadswords with strong, skilled hands, grunting with each swing of the heavy blades and each impact of steel on shield-leather or mail. The fight was slow and brutal, and after a while the warriors could hardly lift their arms.

Owein was the victor in the end: He found an opening and, with a last mighty effort, brought his blade down upon the black knight's helm. The metal cracked; scarlet blood spurted over it and mantled the knight's shoulders. With a cry, the man turned; he stumbled to his horse and, swaying in the saddle, fled.

In the moments it took for Owein t[o]
mount, the black knight disappeared int[o]
the woods fringing the valley. Owein con[-]
tinued in pursuit, however; his hors[e]
pounded through the woods and out th[e]
other side. Ahead, the black horse, with it[s]
broken rider, raced across long water mead[-]
ows, sending up flocks of startled fowl, to[-]
ward a walled and towered city that crowne[d]
a slope far in the distance. The city gate[s]
were open. The black knight, with Owei[n]
now close behind, made for them.

The knight gained the outer gate and dis[-]
appeared through a second gate in the city'[s]
inner curtain wall. Owein galloped throug[h]
the outer portal, but as he passed under th[e]
arch, the iron portcullises in both gate[s]
crashed to the ground. The spikes of th[e]
outer gates stabbed through his horse'[s]
back, and the animal crumpled, screaming[.]
Owein rolled free.

He was trapped in the narrow strip o[f]
land between the two sheer walls. On the fa[r]
side of the inner gate, a road lined wit[h]
houses and thronged with shouting peo[-]
ple swept into the city. A hundred hand[s]
reached up to ease the black knight from hi[s]
horse. Owein leaned against the stones o[f]
the wall and stared through the bars.

His gaze was returned from the othe[r]
side: A woman stood within, a fair youn[g]
maiden robed in white.

"Is it you who wounded the Guardian?" she said in the softest of voices.

"I am the one," he replied. "If yon black knight is he."

"The people will turn on you in a moment. Take this ring now and hold it so that the stone is turned into your hand. It will hide you from them. When they raise the gate, come to me where I stand on yonder horse block. Put your hand on my shoulder to tell me you are there, and I will lead you to refuge."

"Lady, why should you do this?"

"The slayer of the Guardian becomes the new Guardian," said the lady. "My task is to set you in the black knight's place, as lord of the Countess of the Fountain. I am Luned, the lady's servant."

All happened as Luned had said. The mob turned toward the gate where Owein stood beside the broken body of his horse. Screaming, they drew up the inner portcullis and surged into Owein's prison. But they could not see him; the ring protected him. He walked through the jostling throng to the horse block where Luned was. He put his hand lightly on her shoulder. Showing not even a flicker of surprise, she stepped down and began to walk through the town. She led him into the courtyard of the palace that stood at the center of the city and up the winding stair of a tower.

The chamber where Owein sheltered was

fit for a king, hung with scarlet and gray and ornamented with gold. Owein bathed in a tub of bronze beside a charcoal fire; then Luned served him from dishes of silver. She left him, but she returned from time to time to tell him the import of the sounds he heard below: of the great wail that signified the death of the Guardian; of the formal lamentation that meant he had been laid on his bier and carried into the courtyard. From his chamber window, Owein watched the chanting priests, the lords and ladies still as statues on their horses, the trumpeters with their golden horns, and in the center of the crowd, the bier, guarded at head and foot with flaming tapers. The candlelight shone on the hair of the woman who stood beside the bier, a white-faced, golden woman whose wailing sounded high above the trumpets' call.

"That is the Countess of the Fountain," said Luned, at his elbow. "She whose lord you must be. I will take you to her, when the time is right."

For two days and nights, while the black

131

knight's burial rites took place and the lad
mourned, Owein waited in his chambe
served by Luned. On the third day, Lune
led him to her lady.

But the Countess turned her head awa
and would not reach her hand to raise hir
from his knees. "This is the man that reft m
lord's life from his body," she said.

Owein glanced for direction at Lune
The maiden was unmoved by her mistress
words. "What harm is there in that?" sh
said. "He is a better knight than the Guard
ian; your old lord's time had passed. This
your new lord, and new Guardian."

And so it came to be. The Countess c
the Fountain called her lords and baror
together and told them that the new Guard
ian had arrived, and they accepted Owein
Their safety depended on the safety of th
fountain, and they therefore eagerly gree
ed its champion.

For three years, Owein remained with th
lady, protecting with spear and sword th
fountain that held the secret of the land
health. In the words of the chronicler
"Whatever knights came there, Owei
would overthrow them and hold them t
ransom for their full worth; and that wealt
Owein distributed amongst his barons and
knights, so that his dominions had not lov
for a man in the whole world greater tha
their love for him."

He was guardian of the people and hus
band to the lady; his life was one of honor
Images of his own world – of Arthur th
King, of Lancelot and Gawain and his com
panions in arms – faded from his memory
But he was called to his own world again.

A day came when Owein rode forth from
the city in answer to the thunderclap tha
signaled intruders on the fountain ground
As his predecessor had, Owein gallope
across the fields and through the forest int
the valley where the fountain stood. A
knight waited there for him; he unhorse
the man with ease. But this man was no
alone. Within the precincts of the foun
tain was pitched a splendid camp, gay
with silk and ablaze with banners. The
wounded knight stumbled into this en

campment, and his fellows immediately shouted challenges to the victor.

So on the next day, Owein fought another of the company, defeating him; and the next day another; and the next another. But at last a man who seemed to be his equal faced him. These two struggled all through a day and into the night, when the torches were lighted. In the shadows, when both men staggered with exhaustion, Owein knocked his enemy's helm from his head and saw in the torchlight the face of his cousin, Gawain of Orkney.

Owein's sword dropped; he greeted his cousin and named Gawain the victor. Then the companions of the Round Table met again with joy; together, led by King Arthur, they rode to the city of the Countess of the Fountain; together they begged that Owein might leave her for only three months to visit his own country and his own people. The lady gave her consent, said the chroniclers, "but she found it hard."

Owein stayed not three months but three years, for when he was again with Arthur's company and among his kindred, the memory of his lady vanished from his mind. He might have stayed forever, except that one day a strange woman rode into the hall at Arthur's court. She called Owein a traitor for deceiving her lady. Then she vanished.

Some storytellers say that the visitation roused Owein's memory of the other world and drove him mad with remorse. He left Arthur's court then and wandered the desolate mountains, wraithlike and wild, living among the beasts. He was rescued at last by a gentlewoman, whose name has been lost. She took Owein into her own manor and healed him. He departed alone, armed and mounted, to find the lady whose lord he was and the land whose guardian he was.

But the boundaries of other worlds were shifty; the wildernesses were many. Owein rode solitary through many days and nights before he found the way he sought. A lion guided him to it.

It happened this way: As Owein strode along one afternoon, leading his horse to give it a rest, he heard a harsh cough and a

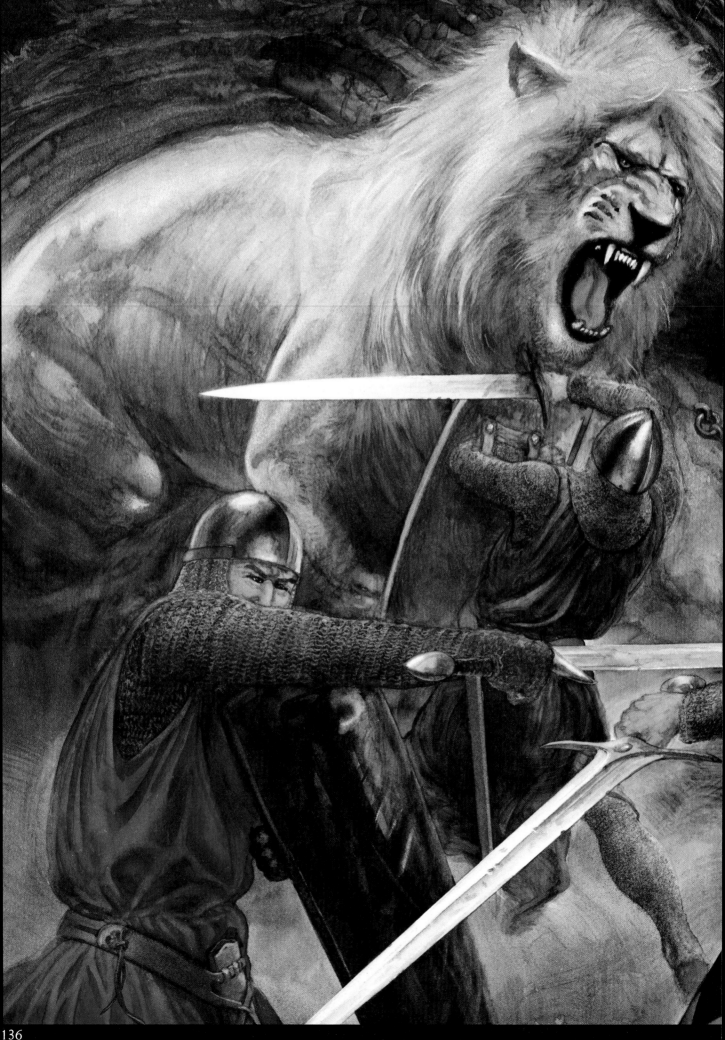

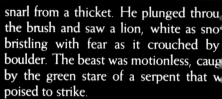

snarl from a thicket. He plunged throu
the brush and saw a lion, white as sno
bristling with fear as it crouched by
boulder. The beast was motionless, caug
by the green stare of a serpent that w
poised to strike.

Swifter than thought, Owein acted. H
sword swept down repeatedly, cleaving t
serpent into twitching pieces. Released, t
white lion bowed its head to him. Wh
Owein left the thicket, the beast followe
It paced beside him as he took up the tra
When night fell and Owein stopped at
clearing in the wood, the lion vanished, la
er returning with a roebuck it had killed.

Owein built a fire and squatted beside
cleaning the game and tossing pieces to th
lion from time to time. As he worked,
moan sounded, and then another. The c
came from a boulder, it seemed.

But the boulder concealed a cave mouth
"Who lies in the cold ground?" calle
Owein. The horse ignored the scene, b
the lion watched alertly.

"Luned lies imprisoned here," came th
answer from the rock.

The knight caught his breath: He mu
be near now, he thought. He asked, "Wh
are you imprisoned thus?"

"I brought my lady a husband and
Guardian for the fountain that protects ou
land. This Guardian left her before his time
three years he has been gone, and the peo
ple say the fault is mine. For the fault I l
here in the cold, until her warriors come t
burn me." The voice trailed into silence.

"I will meet them," Owein said.

And when two men came to drag Lune
from her prison, the knight was waiting. H
sat astride his horse, his shield over hi
shoulder and his sword unsheathed.

The men drew up. They challenged him
He answered in kind, and they attacked.

Owein was weaker than he thought, afte
his long wandering. He was thrown from hi
saddle by the first blow of one warrior'
lance, and the pair of them bore down or
him as he clambered slowly to his feet
But just then, with a roar, the white lior
leaped over Owein's head to the two war

riors. Its great weight dragged them to the ground; its curving claws and fangs ripped into their throats. Within moments, the beast was feasting on their flesh, and its snowy coat was spattered with scarlet. It paid no further attention to Owein, nor to Luned, when Owein freed her.

Then Owein and the servant of the Countess of the Fountain rode together to the lady. She welcomed him with joy and without reproach, for by rules no mortal understood, the thread of her life was entwined with his.

They had some weeks together. And one day, they stood beneath the tree that overspread the fountain Owein guarded, and his lady told him this: He could not stay in her world, for he was a mortal man and would always be drawn to his own.

"Then let us leave it," Owein said. "Your life is tied to mine now. Let another lady reign over the city; let another man guard the fountain."

The lady assented. She left her own world behind and rode away with Owein. It was said that she lived at Arthur's court for the rest of her life.

What became of her country, the story does not tell. After the lady left it, a veil seemed to draw around the place. It was never seen again by mortal eyes. But it may be that it still thrives, sheltered from time and change; it may be that the fountain eternally flows, and a knight eternally guards it, serving a woman who rules a hidden land of Faerie.

Picture Credits

The sources for the illustrations in this book are shown below. When known, the artist's name precedes the picture source.

Cover: Jasper Francis Cropsey (detail), National Gallery of Art, Washington, D.C., Avalon Fund. 1-5: Artwork by Michael Hague. 6-9: Artwork by Susan Gallagher. 12-15: Artwork by John Collier. 18, 19: Artwork by John Jude Palencar. 22, 23: Luminais, Musée des Beaux-Arts, Quimper, France. 24-29: Artwork by Michael Hague. 30: Artwork by Troy Howell. 32-47: Artwork by Gary Kelley. 48-57: Artwork by Troy Howell. 60-67: Artwork by Susan Gallagher. 68: Artwork by Matt Mahurin. 70, 71: Artwork by Susan Gallagher. 74: Artwork by Matt Mahurin. 76-89: Artwork by Willi Glasauer. 90-96: Artwork by Yvonne Gilbert. 98: Artwork by Matt Mahurin. 100-103: Artwork by Michael Hague. 106-113: Artwork by Yvonne Gilbert. 116-119: Artwork by Michael Hague. 120-139: Artwork by John Howe. 144: Artwork by Michael Hague.

Bibliography

Aldington, Richard, and Delano Ames, transls., *New Larousse Encyclopedia of Mythology*. London: The Hamlyn Publishing Group, 1974.

Almgren, Bertil, et al., *The Viking*. Gothenburg, Sweden: AB Nordok, 1975.

Auden, W. H., and Paul B. Taylor, *Norse Poems*. London: The Athlone Press, 1981.

Beck, Horace, *Folklore and the Sea*. Mystic, Connecticut: The Marine Historical Association, 1979.

Branston, Brian, *Gods of the North*. New York: The Vanguard Press, no date.

Briggs, Katharine M.:
An Encyclopedia of Fairies: Hobgoblins, Brownies, Bogies, and Other Supernatural Creatures. New York: Pantheon Books, 1976.*
Folk Narrative. Vol. 1. Part A of *A Dictionary of British Folk-Tales in the English Language*. London: Routledge & Kegan Paul, 1971.

Bulfinch, Thomas, *Bulfinch's Mythology*. New York: Avenel Books, 1979.

Carlyon, Richard, *A Guide to the Gods*. New York: Quill, 1982.

Cavendish, Richard, ed.:
Man, Myth & Magic. 11 vols. New York: Marshall Cavendish, 1983.
Mythology: An Illustrated Encyclopedia. London: Orbis, 1980.

Christiansen, Reidar T., *Studies in Irish and Scandinavian Folktales*. Copenhagen: Rosenkilde and Bagger, 1959.

Croker, Thomas Crofton, *Fairy Legends and Traditions of the South of Ireland*. 3 vols. London: J. Murray, 1825-1828.

Cross, Tom Peete, and Clark Harris Slover, *Ancient Irish Tales*. Totowa, New Jersey: Barnes and Noble, 1981 (reprint of 1936 edition).

d'Arbois de Jubainville, Henri, ed., *Revue Celtique*. Vols. 9 and 10. Paris: F. Vieweg, 1888 and 1889.*

Davidson, Hilda R. Ellis:
Gods and Myths of Northern Europe. New York: Penguin Books, 1982.
The Road to Hel: A Study of the Conception of the Dead in Old Norse Literature. New York: Greenwood Press, 1968.*
Scandinavian Mythology (Library of the World's Myths and Legends series). London: Hamlyn, 1983.

Deane, Tony, and Tony Shaw, *The Folklore of Cornwall*. Totowa, New Jersey: Rowman and Littlefield, 1975.

Duxbury, Brenda, and Michael Williams, *King Arthur Country in Cornwall*. Bodmin, England: Bossiney Books, 1979.

Edda Sæmunder: The Poetic Edda. Transl. by Lee M. Hollander.

Austin, Texas: University of Texas Press, 1962.*

Evans-Wentz, W. Y., *The Fairy-Faith in Celtic Countries*. Secaucus, New Jersey: University Books, 1966.

Farmer, David Hugh, *The Oxford Dictionary of Saints*. Oxford, England: Oxford University Press, 1982.

Folklore, Myths and Legends of Britain. London: The Reader's Digest Association, 1973.

Frazer, Sir James George, *The New Golden Bough*. Ed. by Theodor H. Gaster. New York: The New American Library, 1964.

Froud, Brian, and Alan Lee, *Faeries*. New York: Harry N. Abrams, 1978.

Gold. New York: Alpine Fine Arts Collection, 1981.

Graves, Robert, *The Greek Myths*. Vols. 1 and 2. New York: Penguin Books, 1983.

Gregory, Lady, ed. and transl.:
Cuchulain of Muirthemne: The Story of the Men of the Red Branch of Ulster. Gerrards Cross, England: Colin Smythe, 1979 (reprint of 1902 edition).*
Gods and Fighting Men: The Story of the Tuatha De Danaan and of the Fianna of Ireland. Gerrards Cross, England: Colin Smythe, 1979 (reprint of 1904 edition).*

Grimm, Jacob, *Teutonic Mythology*.

Vol. 3. Transl. by James Steven Stallybrass. Gloucester, Massachusetts: Peter Smith, 1976 (reprint of 1883 edition).

Hamilton, Edith, *Mythology*. New York: The New American Library, 1969.

Hartland, Edwin Sidney, *The Science of Fairy Tales*. Detroit: Singing Tree Press, 1968 (reprint of 1891 edition).*

Heath, Ian, *The Vikings* (Elite series). London: Osprey, 1985.*

Higginson, Thomas Wentworth, *Tales of the Enchanted Islands of the Atlantic*. Great Neck, New York: Core Collection Books, 1976 (reprint of 1898 edition).*

Hveberg, Harald, *Of Gods and Giants: Norse Mythology*. Transl. by Pat Shaw Iversen. Oslo: Tanum-Norli, 1983.

Ions, Veronica:
Egyptian Mythology (Library of the World's Myths and Legends series). New York: Peter Bedrick Books, 1983.
The World's Mythology in Colour. London: Hamlyn, 1974.*

Jacobs, Joseph, ed., *The Book of Wonder Voyages*. New York: Macmillan, 1896.

Johnson, William Branch, *Folktales of Brittany*. London: Methuen, 1927.

Jones, Gwyn, and Thomas Jones, transls., *The Mabinogion*. London: J. M. Dent and Sons, 1976.*

Leach, Maria, ed., *Funk & Wagnalls Standard Dictionary of Folklore, Mythology and Legend*. 2 vols. New York: Funk & Wagnalls, 1949.

Lehane, Brendan, *The Companion Guide to Ireland*. London: William Collins Sons, 1973.

Loomis, Roger Sherman, *Studies in Medieval Literature*. New York: Burt Franklin, 1970.

MacCana, Proinsias, *Celtic Mythology*. London: The Hamlyn Publishing Group, 1970.

MacCulloch, John Arnott:
The Celtic and Scandinavian Religions. Westport, Connecticut: Greenwood Press, 1973.
Eddic. Vol. 2 of *The Mythology of All Races*. New York: Cooper Square, 1964.

Map, Walter, *De Nugis Curialium (Courtiers' Trifles)*. Ed. and transl. by M. R. James. Oxford, England: Oxford University Press, 1983.*

Markale, J., *Celtic Civilization*. London: Gordon & Cremonesi, 1978.

Marwick, Ernest W., *The Folklore of Orkney and Shetland*. London: B. T. Batsford, 1975.

Masson, Elsie, *Folk Tales of Brittany*. Ed. by Amena Pendleton. Philadelphia: Macrae-Smith, 1929.

Munch, Peter Andreas, *Norse Mythology: Legends of Gods and Heroes*. Transl. by Sigurd Bernhard Hustvedt. New York: AMS Press, 1970.

Oskamp, H. P. A., *The Voyage of Máel Dúin*. Groningen, The Netherlands: Wolters-Noordhoff, 1970.*

Parry-Jones, D., *Welsh Legends and Fairy Lore*. Folcroft, Pennsylvania: Folcroft Library Editions, 1976.*

Patch, Howard Rollin:
The Other World. Cambridge, Massachusetts: Harvard University Press, 1950.*
"Some Elements in Mediaeval Descriptions of the Otherworld." *Publications of the Modern Language Association* (Baltimore), 1918.

Paton, Lucy Allen, *Studies in the Fairy Mythology of Arthurian Romance*. New York: Burt Franklin, 1960.

Platt, Colin, *The Abbeys and Priories of Medieval England*. London: Martin Secker & Warburg, 1984.

Ravenel, Florence Leftwich, "Tydorel and Sir Gowther." *Publications of the Modern Language Association* (Baltimore), 1905.*

Rees, Alwin, and Brinley Rees, *Celtic Heritage: Ancient Tradition in Ireland and Wales*. New York: Thames and Hudson, 1961.

Reinhard, John Revell, *The Survival of the Geis in Mediaeval Romance*. Halle, Germany: Max Niemeyer, 1933.

Rhys, John, *Celtic Folklore: Welsh and Manx*. New York: Arno Press, 1980 (reprint of 1901 edition).

Rolleston, T. W., *Myths & Legends of the Celtic Race*. London: George G. Harrap, 1911.

Ross, Anne, *Pagan Celtic Britain: Studies in Iconography and Tradition*. London: Routledge and Kegan Paul, 1967.

Rydberg, Viktor, *Teutonic Mythology*. London: Swan Sonnerschein, 1891.

Saxo Grammaticus:
The History of the Danes. Vol. 1, transl. by Peter Fisher. Vol. 2, ed. and transl. by Hilda R. Ellis Davidson and Peter Fisher. Totowa, New Jersey: Rowman and Littlefield, 1980.*
The Nine Books of the Danish History of Saxo Grammaticus. Vols. 1 and 2. Transl. by Lord Oliver Elton. London: Norrœna Society, 1905.

Sharkey, John, *Celtic Mysteries: The Ancient Religion*. New York: Thames and Hudson, 1979.

Squire, Charles, *Celtic Myth & Legend: Poetry & Romance*. North Hollywood, California: Newcastle, 1975 (reprint of 1905 edition).

Vergil:
The Aeneid: An Epic Poem of Rome. Transl. by L. R. Lind. Bloomington, Indiana: Indiana University Press, 1962.*
The Aeneid of Virgil. Transl. by Allen Mandelbaum. New York: Bantam Books, 1971.*

Yeats, W. B., ed., *Fairy and Folk Tales of Ireland*. London: Pan Books, 1981.

* *Titles marked with an asterisk were particularly helpful in the preparation of this volume.*

Acknowledgments

The editors thank the following for their help in the preparation of this volume: Rolf Andrée, Kunstmuseum, Düsseldorf; François Avril, Curator, Département des Manuscrits, Bibliothèque Nationale, Paris; André Cariou, Curator, Musée des Beaux-Arts, Quimper, France; Jen Coxsey, Publications Department, City Museum and Art Gallery, Birmingham, England; Kitty Cruft, Royal Commission on Ancient Monuments, Edinburgh; Danmarks Paedagogiske Bibliotek, Copenhagen; Margit Engström, First Librarian, Vitterhetsakademiens Bibliotek, Stockholm; Clark Evans, Rare Book and Special Collections Division, Library of Congress, Washington, D.C.; Marielise Göpel, Archiv für Kunst und Geschichte, West Berlin; Claus Hansmann, Stockdorf; Christine Hofmann, Bayerische Staatsgemäldesammlungen, Munich; Heidi Klein, Bildarchiv Preussischer Kulturbesitz, West Berlin; Bernd Krimmel, Mathildenhöhe, Darmstadt; Kunsthistorisches Institut der Universität, Bonn; Françoise Mestre, Jacana, Paris; Luisa Ricciarini, Milan; Justin Schiller, New York City; Robert Shields, Rare Book and Special Collections Division, Library of Congress, Washington, D.C.; Julian Spalding, Director, City Art Gallery, Manchester, England; Lena Törnqvist, Librarian, Svenska Barnboksinstitutet, Stockholm; Stephen Wildman, Deputy Keeper (Fine Art), City Museum and Art Gallery, Birmingham, England.

Time-Life Books Inc.
is a wholly owned subsidiary of

TIME INCORPORATED

FOUNDER: Henry R. Luce 1898-1967

Editor-in-Chief: Henry Anatole Grunwald
President: J. Richard Munro
Chairman of the Board: Ralph P. Davidson
Corporate Editor: Ray Cave
Group Vice President, Books: Reginald K. Brack Jr.
Vice President, Books: George Artandi

TIME-LIFE BOOKS INC.

EDITOR: George Constable
Executive Editor: George Daniels
Editorial General Manager: Neal Goff
Director of Design: Louis Klein
Director of Editorial Resources: Phyllis K. Wise
Editorial Board: Dale M. Brown, Roberta
Conlan, Ellen Phillips, Gerry Schremp,
Donia Ann Steele, Rosalind Stubenberg,
Kit van Tulleken, Henry Woodhead
Director of Research and Photography: John
Conrad Weiser

PRESIDENT: William J. Henry
Senior Vice President: Christopher T. Linen
Vice Presidents: Stephen L. Bair, Edward Brash,
Ralph J. Cuomo, Robert A. Ellis, John M.
Fahey Jr., Juanita T. James, James L. Mercer,
Wilhelm R. Saake, Robert H. Smith, Paul R.
Stewart, Leopoldo Toralballa

THE ENCHANTED WORLD

SERIES DIRECTOR: Ellen Phillips
Deputy Editor: Robin Richman
Designer: Dale Pollekoff
Series Administrator: Jane Edwin

Editorial Staff for *Fabled Lands*
Text Editor: Tony Allan
Researcher: Myrna Traylor-Herndon
Assistant Designer: Lorraine D. Rivard
Copy Coordinators: Barbara Fairchild
Quarmby, Robert M. S. Somerville
Picture Coordinator: Bradley Hower
Editorial Assistant: Constance B. Strawbridge

Editorial Operations
Copy Chief: Diane Ullius
Editorial Operations: Caroline A.
Boubin (manager)
Production: Celia Beattie
Quality Control: James J. Cox (director)
Library: Louise D. Forstall

Correspondents: Elisabeth Kraemer-Singh
(Bonn); Dorothy Bacon (London); Miriam
Hsia (New York); Maria Vincenza Aloisi,
Josephine du Brusle (Paris); Ann Natanson
(Rome). Valuable assistance was also
provided by: Gevene Hertz (Copenhagen);
Lance Keyworth (Helsinki); Judy Aspinall,
Millicent Trowbridge (London); Felix
Rosenthal (Moscow); Dag Christensen
(Oslo); Mary Johnson (Stockholm).

Chief Series Consultant

Tristram Potter Coffin, Professor of
English at the University of Pennsylvania, is a leading authority on folklore.
He is the author or editor of numerous
books and more than one hundred articles. His best-known works are *The British Traditional Ballad in North America, The Old Ball Game, The Book of Christmas Folklore* and *The Female Hero.*

This volume is one of a series that is based
on myths, legends and folk tales.

Other Publications:

UNDERSTANDING COMPUTERS
YOUR HOME
THE KODAK LIBRARY OF CREATIVE PHOTOGRAPHY
GREAT MEALS IN MINUTES
THE CIVIL WAR
PLANET EARTH
COLLECTOR'S LIBRARY OF THE CIVIL WAR
THE EPIC OF FLIGHT
THE GOOD COOK
WORLD WAR II
HOME REPAIR AND IMPROVEMENT
THE OLD WEST

For information on and a full description
of any of the Time-Life Books series listed
above, please write:
Reader Information
Time-Life Books
541 North Fairbanks Court
Chicago, Illinois 60611

Library of Congress Cataloguing in
Publication Data
Main entry under title:
Fabled lands.
   (The Enchanted world)
   Bibliography: p.
   1. Geographical myths.   2. Voyages to
the other world.   3. Tales.
I. Time-Life Books.   II. Series.
GR650.F33 1986   398.2'34   85-28972
ISBN 0-8094-5254-5 (lib. bdg.)
ISBN 0-8094-5253-7 (ret. ed.)